BOTS!

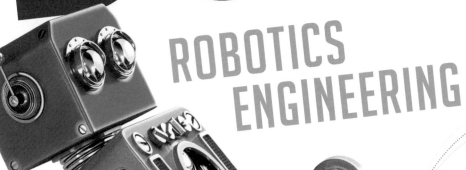

ROBOTICS ENGINEERING

WITH HANDS-ON MAKERSPACE ACTIVITIES

KATHY CECERI

ILLUSTRATED BY LENA CHANDHOK

More engineering titles in the **Build It Yourself** series.

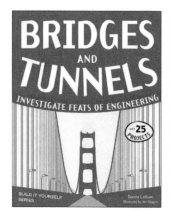

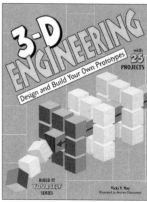

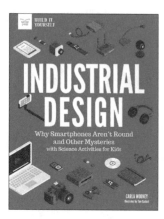

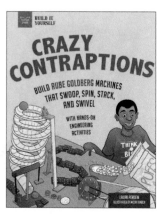

Check out more titles at www.nomadpress.net

Nomad Press

A division of Nomad Communications

10 9 8 7 6 5 4 3 2 1

This book was manufactured by Versa Press, East Peoria, Illinois
October 2019, Job #J19-06343
ISBN Softcover: 978-1-61930-830-5
ISBN Hardcover: 978-1-61930-827-5

Educational Consultant, Marla Conn

Questions regarding the ordering of this book should be addressed to
Nomad Press
2456 Christian St., White River Junction, VT 05001
www.nomadpress.net

Printed in the United States.

CONTENTS

Interested in Primary Sources? Look for this icon.

Use a smartphone or tablet app to scan the QR code and explore more! Photos are also primary sources because a photograph takes a picture at the moment something happens. You can find a list of URLs on the Resources page. If the QR code doesn't work, try searching the internet with the Keyword Prompts to find other helpful sources.

🔎 robotics

200 BCE. A mechanical musical group is presented to the Chinese emperor.

1464 CE. Italian artist and inventor Leonardo da Vinci designs a mechanical knight at age 12.

1822 . . . English mathematician Charles Babbage creates a mechanical calculator called the Analytical Engine.

1842 . . . English writer Ada Lovelace designs an early computer program for Charles Babbage's invention.

1921 . . . Writer Karel Capek from Czechoslovakia invents the word *robot* in his play *R.U.R.*

1947 . . . The invention of the transistor makes small, light, movable computers and robots possible.

1961 . . . Unimate, the first robot used in a factory, is installed in a General Motors automobile plant in New Jersey.

1971 . . . Cheap, compact microprocessors make it possible to add computing ability to almost any kind of electric device.

1986 . . . Honda begins work on a walking robot, the first ASIMO.

1997 . . . The IBM chess-playing robot Deep Blue wins against chess master Garry Kasparov.

1999 . . . Intuitive Surgical introduces the da Vinci Surgical System, which helps doctors operate using miniature medical tools.

2002 . . . The first popular home robot, the Roomba vacuum cleaner, is sold by iRobot.

2004 . . . The NASA robot rovers *Spirit* and *Opportunity* begin exploring the planet Mars.

2010 . . . Google tests a self-driving car on roads in California.

2011 . . . After a massive earthquake in Japan, iRobot PackBots are sent in to investigate a flood-damaged nuclear power plant.

2011 . . . The IBM computer Watson beats two top human players on the TV game show *Jeopardy*.

2012 . . . Hospitals in the United States begin using the ReWalk-powered exoskeleton with patients who are paralyzed.

2013 . . . Harvard demonstrates the first in a line of RoboBees, flying swarm robots designed to help with crop pollination, search-and-rescue missions, and weather monitoring.

2017 . . . A security robot drives itself into a courtyard fountain in a Washington, DC, office complex.

2019 . . . Boston Dynamics releases the SpotMini robot dog for homes and offices. It opens doors and carries objects with its snake-like head.

THE WORLD OF
ROBOTICS

Welcome to the amazing world of robots! Remember the robots from *Star Wars*, *WALL-E*, and *Big Hero 6*? Not that long ago, robots were found only in books and movies. Today, real robots are everywhere!

Robots do many different jobs. Industrial robots assemble huge cars and tiny computer chips. Household robots vacuum floors and mow lawns. Security robots patrol malls and supermarkets. And self-driving robotic cars carry people and packages around town.

ESSENTIAL QUESTION

What task would you ask a robot to do?

Sometimes, robots do dangerous jobs. Firefighting robots equipped with water cannons can go inside burning buildings too hot for humans. Bomb disposal robots protect police and military personnel as well as civilians. We send robots to explore the depths of the ocean and the expanse of space.

BOTS!

But robots don't just do risky, delicate, or boring work for us. Robot toys play with us, follow our commands, and respond to our moods. Robot pets keep people company in nursing homes. Musical robots accompany popular musicians.

Robotics is the science of designing, building, controlling, and **OPERATING ROBOTS**.

This robot, named Pepper, helps in stores, offices, homes, and schools.
Credit: Tokumeigakarinoaoshima (CC BY 1.0)

Creating a robot requires knowledge in **STEM**—Science, **Technology**, **Engineering**, and Math. It takes experts in many different areas to create robots. They include scientists who study plants and animals and the way people think and behave, as well as inventors, builders, designers, and artists. In fact, some people prefer the term STEAM—with an added A for "art."

Robotics is also a popular hobby. Kids and adults enjoy making their own robots from kits or from parts they find themselves. Lots of interesting robot designs have been built by robotics fans working in their own homes or with other people in robotics clubs.

Students at a robotics competition

Robots may be machines, but for many people, the goal is to build robots that act as though they're alive. Maybe one day, we'll have robots that seem almost as human as we are!

WHAT IS A ROBOT, EXACTLY?

The word **ROBOTICS** was first used by science fiction writer Isaac Asimov (1920–1992) in the 1941 book **I, ROBOT**. The title inspired the name of the company **iROBOT**, maker of the Roomba **ROBOTIC VACUUM CLEANER**.

Before you start working on your own robot models, let's learn what makes a robot a robot. If you look in the dictionary, you'll find *robot* defined as a machine that looks and acts like a human being. That description might work for movie robots, but in real life, robots take many forms. Household robotic vacuums look like giant hockey pucks. In a factory, a robot can be just an arm. There are robots in the shape of cars, insects, or even entire houses!

BOTS!

roboticist: a scientist who works with robots.

sense-think-act cycle: a decision-making process used by robots.

sensor: in robotics, a device to detect what's going on outside the machine.

controller: a switch, computer, or microcontroller that can react to what the sensor detects.

effector: a device that lets a robot affect things in the outside world, such as a gripper, tool, laser beam, or display panel.

drive system: wheels, legs, or other parts that make a robot move.

capacitor: an electrical component, such as a battery, that stores an electrical charge and releases it all at once when needed.

smart material: a material that can be used to build robots that react to their surroundings through their bodies.

soft robot: a robot with a flexible or changeable body that helps it respond to its surroundings.

To most **roboticists**, a robot is a machine that can go through the **sense-think-act cycle**.

• **Sense:** to take in information about what is going on around it.

• **Think:** to use that information to select the next step to take.

• **Act:** to do something that affects the outside world.

To complete the sense-think-act cycle, a robot needs to have at least three kinds of parts. A **sensor** detects what's going on, a **controller** reacts to what the sensor detects, and an **effector** can take action. A robot can have many other parts, such as a **drive system** that makes a robot move around and a body to hold the parts together. You'll learn more about the parts of a robot later and get to make some of your own!

Safety First!

Please ask an adult for permission before taking anything apart and to help you with anything hard to open. If you are taking something apart that has an electric cord, first make sure it is unplugged. Then, have an adult cut the cord off and throw it away! Robotics expert Ed Sobey offers the following safety tips.

› Wear eye protection. Safety goggles can be found at hardware stores.

› Before you break something open, see if you can figure out how it was put together and then take it apart the same way.

› If you need to pry something open, push away from yourself.

› When taking apart electrical devices such as cameras, watch out for **capacitors**. Capacitors look like small barrels or batteries with two wire "legs." They are used to store electricity and may give you a powerful shock if you touch the wires. To make capacitors safe, hold onto a screwdriver by the wooden or plastic handle ONLY. Then, tap the metal end of the screwdriver on both "legs" of the capacitor at the same time. If there's a charge, you'll see a little spark as it discharges. Do this a few times until no more sparks appear.

NO BRAINS, NO BODIES

Not all roboticists agree with the sense-think-act definition of a robot. Some believe that a robot is any machine that can act on its own. Even robots that don't have brains can behave in surprisingly lifelike ways. Some move around at random. Others react to their surroundings thanks to bodies made from **smart materials**, such as robots held together by stretchy strings that move in different directions when made to vibrate at different speeds. Robots such as these have programmable bodies that move in different ways depending on their weight and shape. So-called **soft robots** that are made from materials that can squish, stretch, or bend often fall into this category.

BOTS!

WORDS TO KNOW

computer: an electronic device that stores and processes information.

microcontroller: a very small device that works like a mini-computer.

artificial intelligence (AI): the intelligence of a computer, program, or machine.

computer program: a set of steps that tells a computer what to do.

electronic: describes a device that uses computer parts to control the flow of electricity.

circuit: a path that lets electricity flow when closed in a loop.

scavenged: taken from something that is broken or no longer used.

data: information, usually given in the form of numbers, that can be processed by a computer.

device: a piece of equipment, such as a phone, that is made for a specific purpose.

More and more researchers and hobbyists are interested in these simple, behavior-based robots that have no **computers** or **microcontrollers**. They are cheaper and easier to build than robots with controllers. And they can be used as models to help scientists build more complicated robots.

Another branch of robotics focuses on creating **artificial intelligence (AI)**. These are **computer programs** that can understand human language and react in a natural way. AI is what makes it possible to have a conversation with Siri on an iPhone or Alexa on an Amazon Echo.

They don't use their bodies to act in the world as other kinds of robots, but they often have behaviors that make them seem real.

Home **AI DEVICES** such as personal assistants—also known as virtual assistants or smart speakers—are basically **ROBOT BRAINS** in boxes.

MAKE YOUR OWN BOTS!

The activities in this book show you ways to figure out creative solutions to tricky problems. You will experiment with different materials and design new mechanisms. You'll learn how **electronic circuits** work and even try your hand at simple computer programming. When you're done, you'll have some cool robot models that really work!

Most of the activities in this book require no special equipment or tools. You can use ordinary craft materials and **scavenged** parts, such as the following.

Engineering Design Process

Every engineer uses a notebook to keep track of their ideas and their steps in the engineering design process. As you read through this book and do the activities, organize your observations, **data**, and designs in a design worksheet, like the one shown here. When doing an activity, remember that there is no right answer or right way to approach a project. Be creative and have fun!

Problem: What problem are you trying to solve?

Research: Has anything been invented to help solve the problem? What can you learn?

Question: Are there any special requirements for the device? An example of this is a car that must go a certain distance in a certain amount of time.

Brainstorm: What new designs or materials could you try? Go wild!

Prototype: Pick a promising idea and build a model.

Test: Test your prototype and record your observations.

Iterate: Use test results to improve your idea. Repeat the steps to create the best solution possible!

Recycled toys and household devices: Many old items you may find at home, garage sales, or in thrift shops have motors, switches, wiring, batteries, LED lightbulbs, tubing, and pumps that you can reuse. Look for remote-controlled cars and drones, CD or DVD players, and other toys and devices with parts that spin, light up, play music, or talk.

It's easy to find parts to build simple, **DO-IT-YOURSELF ROBOT** models without spending a lot of money.

WORDS TO KNOW

bioengineering: the use of engineering principles applied to biological function to build devices, tools, or machines for a human need.

3-D printer: a machine or printer that creates three-dimensional objects using a range of materials.

For robot bodies, arms, and legs, try wooden, metal, or plastic building sets, such as Tinker Toys, Erector Sets, and Lego bricks. Old containers, bottle caps, jar lids, CDs, and coasters can be used for wheels. Add electronics to old dolls, stuffed animals, or other non-electronic toys. Greeting cards that play music have tiny speakers you can use.

Household and craft materials: Cardboard boxes, plastic containers, foam core boards, and even wood scraps can be turned into robot bodies. Hold them together with bamboo skewers, zipties, wire twists ties, scrapbooking adhesive dots, duct tape, foam tape, and hot glue. Use aluminum foil duct tape (or regular aluminum foil) and old wire for electrical circuits. Change the weight distribution—or just add personality to your robots—with wooden beads, small wooden shapes, pipe cleaners, googly eyes, peel-and-stick foam shapes, pencil erasers and holders, and other home and office supplies.

Robotics and Bioengineering

Bioengineering is the use of mechanical design and technology in health care and medicine. Robotic bioengineers design machines that can help people live better lives. For example, the e-NABLE project connects children who are missing part or all of their hands with people who create custom-designed artificial hands for them, for free, using **3-D printers**. To make the "robot" hand open and close, the child just has to bend their wrist or elbow. The project was started in 2013 by Rochester Institute of Technology professor Jon Schull, and today involves thousands of people around the world.

Student groups, scout troops, and individuals have printed and assembled e-NABLE hands for kids in their communities or across the country. **Watch the creation of these hands at this website.**

🔎 mic 3-D printed arms

You can find supplies in all kinds of places!

Dollar and discount stores: Look for small, cheap, solar garden lights, hand-held electric fans, electric toothbrushes, radios, keychain lights, calculators, toys that make noise, and light-up jewelry. These stores are also a good source of inexpensive tools, such as small screwdrivers and wire cutters, as well as crafts materials, party items, and office supplies that can be used for construction and decoration.

Electronics and hobby shops: Stores that carry model cars, drones, and other DIY electronic parts may carry supplies such as solar panels, servo motors, switches, wire, and batteries.

Robotics, science, and electronics supply websites: Look online for robot kits, circuit boards, and microcontrollers. You'll find suggested sites and products in the Resources section at the back of this book.

Ready to dive in and learn about bots? Let's go!

Essential Questions

Each chapter of this book begins with an essential question to help guide your exploration of robotics. Keep the question in your mind as you read the chapter. At the end of each chapter, use your notebook to record your thoughts and answers.

ESSENTIAL QUESTION

What task would you ask a robot to do?

ROBOT?
OR NOT?

How can you tell whether a machine meets the sense-think-act definition of a robot? One way is to use an **algorithm** to test it. An algorithm is a series of steps to follow. It can help you make decisions based on how you answer certain questions. A computer program is a kind of algorithm that tells a computer how to decide what to do.

An algorithm can be shown in the form of a diagram called a **flowchart**. A flowchart helps you see the steps to follow and what the result will be. Differently shaped boxes represent different actions. An oval means "Start" or "End." A diamond-shaped decision block contains a question that you have to answer. A rectangular process block tells you what action to take. And an arrow shows you what order to go in.

In this activity, you will list data about different kinds of machines that might be robots. Then, you will plug the data for each machine into the flowchart on the following page to figure out if it meets the sense-think-act definition.

1. In your engineering notebook or on your computer, make a list with four columns. Label the columns "Device," "Sensor," "Controller," and "Effector." In the Device column, list some common machines that might qualify as robots, such as these.

* television

* automatic garage door opener

* calculator

* clothes dryer

* automatic supermarket door

* electric toothbrush

* smoke detector

* automatic soap dispenser

2. For the first device, go to the Sensor column. Write down what kind of sensors it has. If it doesn't have any sensors, write "none." Do the same for the Controller and Effector columns. Continue down the list of devices, filling in the answers across each row of columns.

3. **To use the flowchart, start at the oval at the top.** Follow the arrows, answering the questions in the diamond-shaped decision blocks using the data in your list.

Try This!

Use this flowchart to test other devices around your home and school. Can you spot any patterns in your answers?

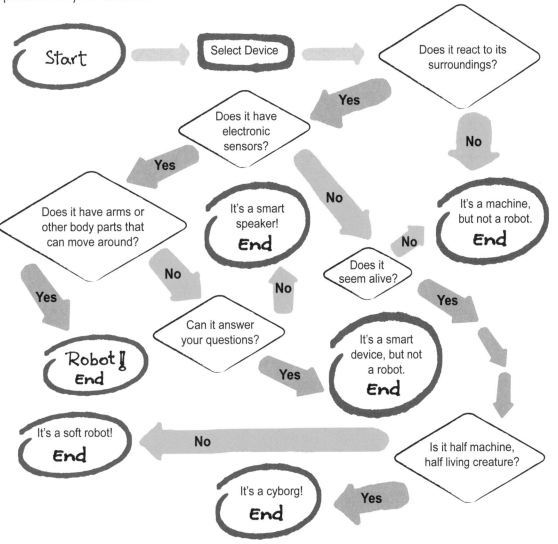

Chapter 1

THE DEVELOPMENT OF
ROBOTICS

Humans have been creating tools to help make work easier since the dawn of time. But robots that can sense, think, and act for themselves have only been possible since the age of electronics began in the middle of the twentieth century. Long before that, programmable automata and other machines were entertaining people and doing work easier and faster than humans can.

As early as 200 **BCE**, a device that used air pipes and ropes pulled by hand to make mechanical musicians play flutes and stringed instruments entertained the emperor of China. More than 1,600 years later, when the famous Italian artist and inventor Leonardo da Vinci (1452–1519) was just 12 years old, he designed a mechanical knight that could sit up and move its arms and head.

ESSENTIAL QUESTION

Which robotic inventions do you think have helped humans the most?

Then, around 1555 CE, an Italian clockmaker named Gianello Torriano (1501–1585) built a wind-up model of a lady that could walk around in a circle while strumming a type of guitar called a lute. You can see the Lute Player Lady in a museum in Vienna, Austria, today.

Soon, inventors started putting **automated** machines to work. In 1801, Joseph Marie Jacquard (1752–1834) built a loom that used chains of **punch cards** to tell it what patterns to weave into the cloth.

WORDS TO KNOW

programmable: able to be provided with coded instructions for the automatic performance of a task.

automata: machines that can move by themselves (singular is automaton).

BCE: put after a date, BCE stands for Before Common Era and counts down to zero. CE stands for Common Era and counts up from zero. These non-religious terms correspond to BC and AD. This book was printed in 2019 CE.

automated: run by machine rather than by people.

punch card: a card with holes punched in it that gives directions to a machine or computer.

radio transmitter: the part of a radio that sends signals.

A Jacquard loom. You can see the punch cards that were used to tell the loom what to do.

In 1898, in New York, New York, the electrical pioneer **NIKOLA TESLA** (1856–1943) showed off the first **REMOTE-CONTROL** device: a mechanical boat controlled by a **radio transmitter**.

Inspired by automated weaving looms, in 1822, English mathematician Charles Babbage (1791–1871) used punch cards in his Analytical Engine, a mechanical calculator. His colleague, Lady Ada Lovelace (1815–1852), designed a series of steps to make the engine solve certain math problems. Her work is considered the world's first computer program.

BOTS!

Research into computerized robots began after World War II. In 1948, mathematician Norbert Wiener (1894–1964) wrote a book called *Cybernetics* that compared the ways people and machines functioned. He found that people and machines both use **feedback**, communication, and control to make decisions and take action.

In 1950, computer scientist Alan Turing (1912–1954) came up with the **Turing test** to see whether a machine was able to think like a human. To pass the test, a computer had to make people think they were talking to a person.

A Robosapien soccer game at a college technology festival in India in 2006. The toy robots were hacked by students from the University of Manitoba Autonomous Agents lab in Canada, which regularly competes in robot sports.

credit: Sancho McCann, flickr.com/photos/
sanchom/502378257/in/photolist-LoPy6-LoCsh-LoPxt

Today, people build, study, and use robots in many different ways. At home, people use robots for their everyday tasks. Government robotics researchers develop rugged robots for use in the military and in scientific exploration. Hobbyists and artists get creative with robots they build themselves from kits, parts, and **salvaged** equipment. And business people work with engineers to make robots less expensive and more useful so that more people and companies will buy them.

When the **ROOMBA** first came out, people began **hacking** the vacuum to see if they could program it themselves. So, the company came out with **CREATE**, a version designed to be hacked. Create robots can play **LASER TAG**, **DANCE**, and even **BE STEERED** by a hamster in a ball attached to the top!

ROBOTICS IN THE HOME

The Roomba vacuum cleaner appeared in stores in 2002. Soon, people were buying over a million Roombas a year. It was the first popular home robot.

Other common household robots include lawn mowers, floor washers, and swimming pool cleaners. Newer robots promise to tidy up a child's messy room or automatically clean the litter box after the cat uses it.

Smart Clothing and Wearable Technology

Wearable technology is the term for "smart" clothes and accessories that have robotic components, such as sensors, processors, and transmitters. For example, the FitBit wristband can track your activity, exercise, sleep, and even weight. Sewable controllers such as the LilyPad Arduino can even be used to create wearable robots! Invented by former MIT professor Leah Buechley, the LilyPad is used to make e-textiles such as clothing that flashes when you twirl around on the dance floor or shoulder bags that blink when you forget to take your keys.

BOTS!

Do you live in a **smart home**? A smart home is a type of robot because it can be programmed to respond to conditions inside and out. Bill Gates (1955–), the founder of the giant computer company Microsoft, built a smart home in 1997 that adjusted the lights, temperature, and music according to the people in the room.

Today, the **Internet of Things (IoT)** can let you see and control what's happening in your home, even when you're not there. IoT devices include doorbells with security cameras, windows and shades that open and close depending on how sunny or dark it is, and washing machines that send alerts to your phone.

Furby!

ROBOTICS IN TOYS

Robotics kits and toys aren't just for kids. Adult hobbyists and researchers use them to build robotic **prototypes** quickly and easily. One of the first programmable robotics kits was the Lego Mindstorms Robotic Invention System. The Mindstorms system uses a simple computer program developed at MIT. Robots are built using Lego bricks, so no tools or wiring are required. Today, robotics kits such as Lego Mindstorms and VEX, which uses metallic parts that screw together, are also used by students in robotics competitions.

Many interactive toys also qualify as "real" robots. They include Furby, a fuzzy, blob-shaped **animatronic** doll that first came out in 1998. Furby could respond by blinking and wiggling its big ears when you tickled it, squeezed it, or gave it a shake. It spoke its own language, Furbish, but "learned" English the longer you owned it.

The Anki Cozmo looked like a miniature bulldozer with a screen for a face. Its built-in camera let it recognize faces and it was able to talk to people or pets by name. The Sphero Star Wars BB-8 Droid is a ball-shaped robot that looks just like the character from *Star Wars*. It also has a personality that adapts to the way you play with. It will even watch and react to *Star Wars* movies.

Both the **BB-8** and the **COZMO** can be programmed using a companion **SMARTPHONE APP**.

Let the Music Play

Musicians use deep learning to create robots that can compose their own music. At the Georgia Tech Center for Music Technology, researchers programmed a robot called Shimon with different styles of music, from classical to jazz. Shimon then played its own songs on the xylophone.

ROBOTICS IN ART

Robots can be programmed to create art. In 2018, the RobotArt competition received 100 robot-created entries by nearly 20 teams from all over the world. The winner was a machine developed by Pindar Van Arman called Cloudpainter, which created portraits from computer images or photos taken by its own camera. Cloudpainter consists of a robotic arm fitted with 3-D-printed paintbrush holder "fingers." It uses AI to combine the image of a person's face with a sample of a real artist's painting to create original works.

BOTS!

WORDS TO KNOW

powered exoskeleton: a "robot suit" that can be worn to give a person added strength.

exoskeleton: a skeleton on the outside of a body.

Robots can also become works of art themselves. A robotic sculpture by Ashley Newton called *Neuroflowers* consisted of giant, clear plastic flowers that could light up, change color, and open and close their petals. At an exhibit in San Francisco, California, in 2015, visitors attached monitors to their bodies to control the flowers using their brain waves and heartbeats.

A working automaton built by **HENRI MAILLARDET** around 1810 is on display at the Franklin Institute in Philadelphia, Pennsylvania. It looks like a boy in a clown's costume, and **CAN DRAW AND WRITE POETRY** in French and English. The machine was the inspiration for the automaton in the book, **THE INVENTION OF HUGO CABRET** by Brian Selznick, and the movie, **HUGO**.

ROBOTICS IN MEDICINE

In hospitals, robots do everything from carry medicines to patients' rooms to help doctors perform surgery!

The da Vinci Surgical System helps surgeons work with miniature tools that make smaller cuts, so the patient can heal more quickly. The machine has four arms that can move in more directions than a human arm. A doctor controls the machine using a 3-D video magnifier screen.

Robots also help patients in their daily lives. Wheelchair-user Amit Goffer of Argo Medical Technologies in Israel developed the ReWalk, a **powered exoskeleton** that helps paralyzed people stand up and walk. Using motorized braces that are strapped onto the user's legs, the ReWalk moves when the person leans forward or backward.

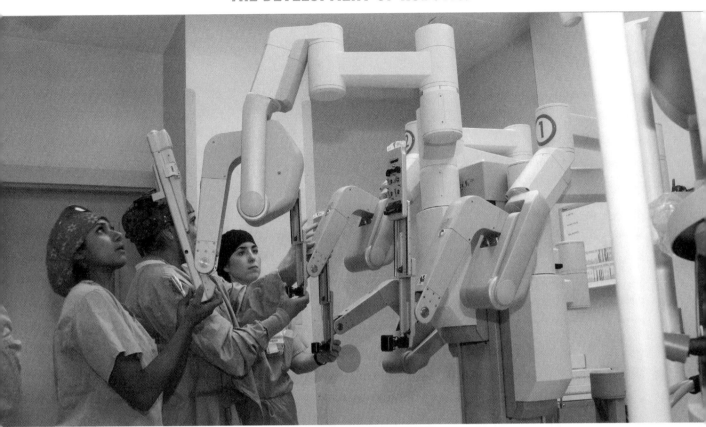

Health care professionals take a look at the da Vinci system.

credit: Mr. Jeff L Troth (Army Medicine)

Dean Kamen

Inventor Dean Kamen (1951–) is known as the founder of the FIRST robotics competition for students. But he got his start making inventions to help people with medical problems. In 1976, he created a robotic syringe that patients can wear. The device automatically gives them shots of drugs whenever they need them. He also created the Segway, a two-wheeled motorized scooter that uses robotic sensors to help it balance even when not in motion. Segways are popular with police, security guards, and tourists.

ROBOTIC SYSTEMS help **FLYING DRONES** stay in the air, keep riders upright on **ELECTRONIC UNICYCLES**, and help you stay aboard your **MOTORIZED SKATEBOARD**.

WORDS TO KNOW

hybrid: something that combines two different things, such as a car that can use two different kinds of devices to power it.

clean room: a room in a laboratory or factory where objects that must be kept free of dust or dirt are made.

plasma torch: a tool that uses streams of electrified gas to cut through sheets of metal.

drone: a plane, quadcopter, or other aircraft that can be controlled by a pilot on the ground.

defuse: to prevent something from exploding.

Fanuc is a Japanese **FACTORY THAT** can operate for a **WHOLE MONTH** with no humans— just robots!

ROBOTICS IN INDUSTRY

Automobile factories and other businesses use robots to do all kinds of dirty, dangerous, boring, or difficult jobs that human workers can't do or don't want to do. The first industrial robot, Unimate, was only a robotic arm. It worked in a General Motors automobile plant in New Jersey in 1961.

Many robotic features can be found in cars today. In 2006, Lexus came out with an Advanced Parking Guidance System that lets a car park itself. Sensors on the wheels use sound waves to tell the car's computer how much space it has.

The 2010 Toyota Prius is a **hybrid** car with computers that switch the motor from gas to electrical power. It also has a self-parking feature.

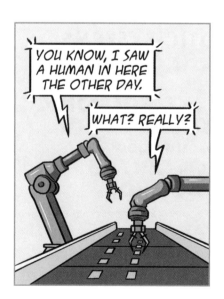

Robots are used in factories that make delicate computer parts, because they don't carry dirt or dust into the **clean room**. "Pick-and-place" robots take materials from one spot on an assembly line and move them somewhere else. Unlike people, they can work long hours without getting tired. That means they are less likely than humans to make mistakes due to exhaustion.

TODAY'S ROBOTIC arms use **plasma torches** TO CUT THROUGH sheets of metal.

MILITARY USE AND DISASTER RESPONSE

Remote-control robots are becoming increasingly important as military tools. **Drones** can be operated by pilots halfway around the world using keyboards and joysticks. Sensors and other on-board electronics help the drones fly on their own, while pilots focus on telling them where to go and what to do, such as take photos.

On the ground, military robots **defuse** bombs and check dangerous areas for hazards. Some look like miniature tanks and can fire machine guns or less harmful weapons, such as bean bags, smoke, and pepper spray.

This robot is part of the U.S. Army's bomb disposal strategy.

BOTS!

radiation: energy in the form of waves or particles.

centaur: a mythical creature with the lower body of a horse and the head and upper body of a human.

telepresence: technology that allows a person in one place to take part in activities somewhere else, using a robot that can let them hear, see, move around, and talk.

augmented reality (AR): technology that adds images or text over a view of an actual place viewed through a device such as a smartphone camera.

hydrothermal vent: an opening in the ocean floor that releases hot gases and minerals from underground.

NASA: National Aeronautics and Space Administration. The U.S. organization in charge of space exploration.

One robot, the TALON, can climb stairs, go over rock piles and barbed wire, plow through snow, and even travel short distances underwater. Its sensors can detect explosives, poisonous gas, harmful **radiation**, and weapons.

In 2018, Italian researchers developed an improved disaster response robot called the Centauro. It looks like a **centaur**, with a body like a horse and human-like arms that let it climb stairs and use regular tools. It can be controlled by a person wearing a full-body **telepresence** suit and using **augmented reality (AR)** techniques.

ROBOTICS IN EARTH EXPLORATION

Scientists use robots to explore regions where people can't go, but it's dangerous work, even for a robot! In 1993, researchers from Carnegie Mellon University accidentally dropped an eight-legged robot called Dante into a volcano in Antarctica. The next year, they had more luck exploring a volcano in Alaska with Dante II. That robot sent back readings from the volcano before it, too, disappeared down the crater.

An underwater robot called ABE helped scientists at the Woods Hole Oceanographic Institution observe the ocean's depths from 1996 until 2010, when it was lost at sea. ABE could dive down more than 14,000 feet without having to be connected to a ship or submarine. That meant ABE could work faster, cheaper, and in more places than other research tools.

ABE helped locate, map, and photograph many deep-sea **hydrothermal vent** sites and volcanoes. It also took magnetic readings that helped scientists understand how the earth's crust was formed. Woods Hole scientists now use a robot called Sentry, which can go even faster and deeper than ABE.

ROBOTICS IN SPACE

Water on Mars

The Mars rover *Spirit* made its greatest discovery because of a broken wheel. In 2007, *Spirit's* broken wheel scraped up some bright-white soil. This dirt was made up of a mineral called silica left behind by water in the form of hot springs or steam. To scientists, this is evidence that life could be possible on Mars.

Robots and outer space have always gone together, both in science fiction and real life. In 1997, **NASA** sent the robotic rover *Sojourner* to Mars on the Pathfinder Mission. The solar-powered robot sent back pictures and analyzed the chemistry of Martian rocks and soil.

The Mars rover *Curiosity* takes a selfie on Mars
credit: NASA/JPL-Caltech/MSSS

BOTS!

The NASA robot rovers *Spirit* and *Opportunity* landed on Mars in 2004. Although they were expected to last only 90 days, *Spirit* lasted until 2010. *Opportunity* kept going until a dust storm on Mars blocked it from recharging its solar batteries. NASA scientists sadly declared *Opportunity* dead in January 2019. The rover lasted 15 years longer than expected and set the record for most distance covered on another planet.

In 2013, sisters Camille and Genevieve Beatty, then ages 13 and 10, built a **FUNCTIONING MODEL OF A MARS ROVER** for the New York **HALL OF SCIENCE**.

In 2012, NASA sent up a bigger, more advanced rover called *Curiosity*. NASA's *Mars 2020 Rover* was based on *Curiosity*'s design. It is about the size of a small car and equipped with drills to collect rock samples. Its mission is to look for signs of past microscopic life—and to test out new technologies that could help future astronauts explore the planet.

Robots have also served on the International Space Station in orbit around Earth. Since 2001, the Canadarm2 robotic arm, built by the Canadian Space Agency, has helped astronauts move large objects and do repairs and experiments outside the ship. Robonaut 2 (R2), the first **humanoid** robot in space, was activated on the space station in 2011. Developed with the help of car-maker General Motors, R2 originally consisted of just a head, body, and two arms.

Learn more about the *Mars 2020 Rover* and mission here.

🔎 NASA Mars 2020

PS

Does a robotic arm need a face? Does a smart home need legs? A robot's job decides the way a robot will look. This is its housing. We'll take a closer look at different kinds of robot housing in the next chapter!

ESSENTIAL QUESTION

Which robotic inventions do you think have helped humans the most?

ARTBOTS
EVERYWHERE!

A vibrating robot usually doesn't have a brain, but it can be designed to act like it does! A motor spins a weight to make it shake, jiggle, and hop along. Depending on how it is balanced, it might spin in overlapping circles or move forward in a zigzagging line. When it touches a wall, it turns and keeps on going. Your ArtBot lets you see how it moves because its legs are markers. Set it on a sheet of paper and it skitters along, drawing as it goes.

SAFETY NOTE: Ask an adult to help with the hot glue gun.

1. If your motor doesn't have wires attached, use wire cutters to cut two pieces of wire about 4 to 6 inches long. Remove about ½ inch of insulation from each end so that the metal inside is exposed. Attach one wire to each of the metal terminals coming out of the motor so that metal touches metal. Secure with electrical tape.

2. Test the motor by touching the other end of the wires to the ends of a battery. If you have a good connection, the **shaft** of the motor will start to turn.

3. Turn the cup upside down. Attach the motor to the bottom of the cup with the foam tape so that the wires stick out either side. The motor shaft can point up or hang over the side of the cup. Use electrical tape to help hold it on.

4. Put a rubber band around the battery so it covers the ends. Wrap tape around the middle of the battery to hold it in place. Use tape to attach the battery next to the motor. Cover it with more electrical tape to help hold it on.

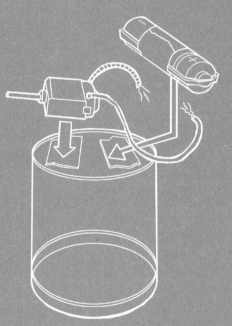

WORDS TO KNOW

shaft: a short rod on a motor that spins.

continued on next page . . .

5. **Stick the ends of the wires under the rubber band.** Make sure the bare wire touches the metal ends of the battery. The motor shaft should turn. If not, move the wires around until it does. Turn the motor on and off by taking out one of the wires. Tape the other wire in place.

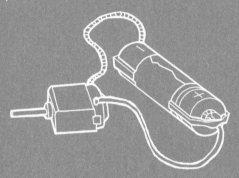

6. **To make an off-balance weight that will shake the cup, stick a cork onto the motor shaft.** To adjust the way the ArtBot shakes, use hot glue to attach a craft stick or small wooden shapes, beads, etc., onto the cork. Make sure the cork and any other weight is uneven as it spins around. If the cork pops off, squeeze a tiny dab of hot glue into the hole for the shaft.

7. **To attach the "legs," hold the markers against the cup with the caps pointing out.** Line up the bottom of the caps with the edge of the cup. Secure with two strips of tape.

8. **Decorate your robot!** Remember that the weight you add will change how the ArtBot moves.

9. **Test out your ArtBot on a large sheet of paper.** What does it do? How does it make art?

Troubleshooting Tips

› Check that the metal ends of the wire are touching the metal ends of the battery. (For more on how circuits work, see Chapter 3 on page 39).

› If the wires, battery, or motor shake themselves loose, add more tape!

› Make sure the spinning motor shaft, cork, and anything connected to them are not rubbing against anything else.

› To change the way the ArtBot moves or to make it lighter, remove or reposition some decorations.

Chapter 2

ROBOTIC
SHAPES AND JOBS

Robots come in every shape and size imaginable. They range from microscopic medical bots to giant automated cranes. And they can be made out of almost any kind of material, from stretchy rubber to rigid steel.

Robot designers have to decide which materials will work best for the machine they want to build. Will the robot need to be heavy to withstand a pounding? Should it be as light as possible to save on the energy it needs to move? Does it have to be rigid enough to carry a heavy load? Or should it be flexible and bendy? Will the robot be working under extreme conditions and need a sturdy metal or plastic framework and covering?

Many industrial, military, and exploration robots look like everyday tools or vehicles.

ESSENTIAL QUESTION

How does a robot's body help it do its job?

Robot toys and **social robots** often look like stuffed animals or friendly, imaginary creatures. Drones resemble miniature helicopters. And humanoid robots can look so real, they're scary! But no matter what it looks like, a robot's outsides are important, because its body determines what it can do.

BIG ROBOTS, LITTLE ROBOTS

Robots vary greatly in size and strength. For example, giant, experimental, self-driving farm tractors use GPS to steer across vast fields, day and night. Their sensors check the moisture level of the soil and alert human controllers to obstacles in the field. Then there's the Semi-Automated Mason (or SAM), a wall-building bot that can lay 3,000 bricks in one day using a conveyer belt and robotic arm.

At the other extreme, **nanobots** are robots that are too small to see without a microscope. At the 2009 RoboCup competition, nanobots played soccer in a stadium the size of a grain of rice.

A group of small robots that work together like ants in an anthill is known as a **swarm**. Just like real insects, swarming robots don't need a lot of brainpower. They know where to move and what to do by following the rest of the group.

In 2018, a team of scientists from Arizona State University and China used **NANOBOTS** to **ATTACK CANCER CELLS** in mice.

The "Uncanny Valley"

Have you ever noticed that some of the most realistic-looking robots are also the creepiest? According to scientists, there's a place between believable and not-quite-believable that gives many people the willies. They call it the **Uncanny Valley**. Researchers don't know why it happens, but one idea is that being afraid of others who don't "look right" helped early humans avoid danger. Some robot makers don't worry about the Uncanny Valley. Artist and engineer David Hanson (1969–) of Hanson Robotics, who helped design animatronic models for Disney, makes humanoid robots that look very realistic. They talk, smile, and even make jokes in a very natural way, thanks to AI brains and special artificial skin called Frubber.

In 2011, a research team from Harvard University developed the Kilobot, an inexpensive, vibrating robot about the size of a quarter. Using sensors that tell them how close they are to their neighbors, Kilobots can be programmed to move in swarms of more than 1,000. Researchers use Kilobots to see how swarms of larger robots might work together to accomplish big tasks.

Modular robots are similar to swarms. Each one is a separate moving robot that can communicate with the others. But modular robots can also join together in different combinations to form a larger robot.

Watch Kilobots form different patterns by following a few simple commands.

🔎 Harvard Kilobots

PS

The SMORES robot from the ModLab at the University of Pennsylvania is made up of small building blocks with wheels. SMORES stands for Self-Assembling MOdular Robot for Extreme Shapeshifting. The blocks can attach to each other and pull apart using **electromagnets**. Robots that can rearrange themselves like real-life Transformers or repair themselves on the go could be handy on space missions and in other hard-to-reach places.

WORDS TO KNOW

biomimetic: a machine or material that copies a living thing.

crop: a plant grown for food or other uses.

pollination: transferring pollen from the male part of a flower to the female part so that the flower can make seeds.

biohybrid: a robot with living material added to it.

ROBOT CRITTERS

When roboticists want their machines to act like living things, they borrow ideas from nature. A **biomimetic** robot is based on an animal, plant, or other life form. In 1995, engineers at the Massachusetts Institute of Technology (MIT) tested the fish-shaped RoboTuna to help with the design of autonomous mini-submarines.

The robotics company Boston Dynamics creates **FOUR-LEGGED ROBOTS** that look and move like real dogs. In 2019, it released its **SPOTMINI DOG**, which has a snake-like head that opens **doors and carries objects.** What would you do with a robotic pet?

A robotic fish from 2010!

credit: Kuba Bozanowski (CC BY 2.0)

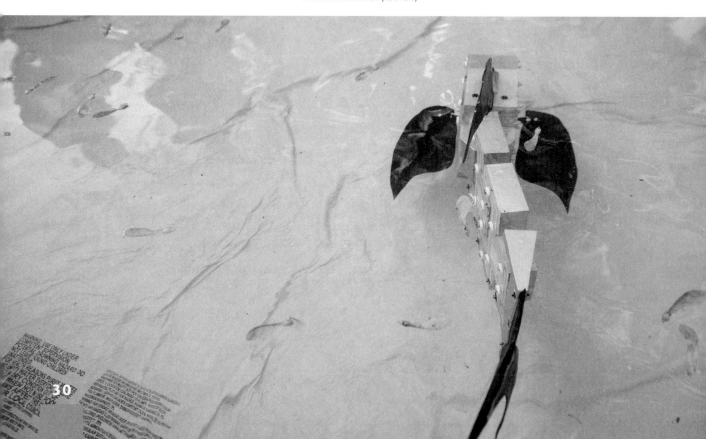

In 2018, a new MIT robot fish called SoFi used a swim bladder similar to that of real fish. It helped the robot swim by moving air in and out of special compartments.

Many biomimetic robots look like bugs. In 2007, DARPA asked scientists to come up with a soft robot that could squeeze through tight openings. Some of these robots looked and moved like caterpillars, inchworms, and slugs. In 2013, Harvard demonstrated the first in a line of RoboBees, flying swarm robots designed to help with **crop pollination**, search-and-rescue missions, and weather monitoring.

At the University of California at Berkeley in 2008, researchers designed a tiny, six-legged robot called Dash that could scamper across the floor as quickly as a cockroach. They turned their design into an educational robot toy called Kamigami, which came with different bodies, including ladybugs and scorpions.

Researchers at the University of Tokyo in Japan created **biohybrid** robotic fingers using living muscle tissue from rats. The tissue was grown from cells and attached to metal and plastic skeletons. Electrical signals made the muscles bend or straighten the fingers. **Take a look at this different kind of robot at this website.**

⌕ NatGeo robotic living muscle

PS

WORDS TO KNOW

laser-cut: cut with a laser cutter, a programmable machine that uses a focused beam of powerful light to burn through wood, paper, metal, or other materials.

pneubotics: inflatable robots made of air.

open source: a computer program or device that makes its design information public so that others can help improve the design and make their own versions.

MATERIALS MAKE A DIFFERENCE

Robot builders often construct their prototypes out of everyday materials that are cheap and easy to work with. This way, they can make changes and new versions quickly. Dash, the robotic cockroach, was made out of **laser-cut** cardboard. That helped Dash survive falls from the tops of buildings. Other researchers make plastic copies on 3-D printers.

One of the finalists in the 2018 Broadcom Masters student science competition was an underwater robot built from PVC plumbing pipes. Sixth-grader Anna Du designed the remote-operated vehicle (ROV) with sensors that can detect small particles of plastics. Her design may someday help scientists clean up ocean pollution.

See Anna Du's underwater robot at this website.

Smithsonian robot microplastics

PS

Want a really lightweight robot? Fill it with air! Around 2011, engineer Saul Griffith (1974–) of Otherlab in San Francisco made an inflatable robot prototype out of a rubber bicycle tube that cost $5. He went on to make **pneubotics** (*pneu* means "air") that walk and move using bubble muscles that fill and empty as needed. Some versions are big and strong enough to ride on!

Kamigami
credit: Collision Conf (CC BY 2.0)

Developing a robot skin that's tough, soft, and sensitive is another challenge for scientists. In 2018, a team led by Zhenan Bao (1970–), a professor of chemical engineering at Stanford University in California, demonstrated a rubber glove that could help robots "feel." The fingertips of the glove were covered in soft electronic skin, or e-skin. The e-skin contained pressure sensors that could send signals to a robot's brain, similar to the nerves in human skin.

When the team put the e-skin glove on a **HEAVY ROBOT HAND**, the robot was able to **GENTLY POKE** a delicate raspberry without squishing it.

That same year, Yale University researchers created a different kind of electronic skin that wrapped around ordinary objects and turned them into moving, grasping robots. In tests, it made a foam tube crawl like an inchworm and a stuffed toy horse walk.

Now that we've examined how a robot's body and materials affects what it can do, it's time to learn more about how robots do what they do.

ESSENTIAL QUESTION

How does a robot's body help it do its job?

Meet RobotGrrl!

At age 13, Canadian entrepreneur Erin Kennedy began building robots on her own with Lego Mindstorms. She soon became known on the web as RobotGrrl. In 2008, she paid for a summer program in AI at Stanford University in California with money earned by making toy vibrating Styrobots from foam drinking cups. After college, Erin's educational robot RoboBrrd won awards at Maker Faires around North America. She designed its body from craft materials such as wooden craft sticks, felt, and feathers.

More recently, Erin created Robot Missions, an **open source** project to work with the public to design, build, and test small robots that clean beach debris. **Watch videos and read interviews about Erin here.**

🔎 robot missions

Robot Test Platform

Robotics hobbyists and researchers often save time by using a pre-built platform. Having a base to work from makes it easier to try different parts and codes. Some use complete robot bodies, such as the Roomba Create, which is based on the design of the robotic vacuum. Others let you add your own components, such as servo motors and sensors.

For some projects, the best (and most fun) option is to build your own! Use the suggestions below to design your own basic robot body. You can also try different materials to make the other robot projects in this book. Be sure to take pictures and keep notes on your materials and designs in your robotics journal so you have a record of what works and what needs improvement.

Body

› Metal: recycled cans and containers, such as Altoid mint tins (make sure no bare wires or batteries touch the metal or you'll cause a short circuit; see Chapter 3)

› Expanded plastic foam: Styrofoam cups or plates, recycled food trays or packing material, cut-up pool noodles, other floating toys

› Paper or cardboard: corrugated cardboard from shipping boxes, cereal boxes, milk cartons

› Stiff plastic: milk jugs, food containers, old plastic toys, DVDs

› Rubber or soft stretchable plastic: inflatable toys, balloons, dog chew toys, bubble wrap

› Wood: craft sticks and shapes, bamboo chopsticks or BBQ skewers, paint stirrers, tree branches

› Soft fabric: stuffed animals, felt

› Wheels and gears

› Kits: Lego, K'Nex

› Repurposed: toy cars or other rolling toys, such as pull-back spring or remote control vehicles. See the Introduction for tips on dismantling old electrical devices

› DIY: bottle caps, lids, coasters, DVDs

Connectors

› Glue: hot glue, adhesive dots

› Strips: plastic zip ties, twist ties, pipe cleaners, wire, hook and latch strips such as Velcro

› Tape: clear, electrical, foam, duct

› Other: paper clips, binder clips, nuts and bolts, brads

MAKE YOUR OWN
ROBOT SKIN

TOOLBOX!
- 4 tablespoons glycerin
- 4 tablespoons gelatin (unflavored or sugar-free)
- slightly more than 3 tablespoons hot water
- plastic bowl or other mold
- small microwavable container
- microwave oven

Roboticists turn to chemistry when they want to create new kinds of soft robot bodies. This edible robotic material is made using glycerin (a sugary syrup sold in pharmacies as a skin moisturizer and in health food stores as a sweetener) and gelatin dessert mix. In this project, mix up your own non-toxic robot material, and in the next project, mold it to create an inflatable robot. It's very stretchy!

SAFETY NOTE:

Be careful when handling hot water or gelatin—have an adult help.

Don't eat your robot (or any science experiment)! To make a small sample to taste, use only food-grade glycerin and mold it separately in a clean plastic cup.

Avoid getting colored gelatin on your clothing, as it might stain.

1. **Measure the glycerin into a microwavable container.** Sprinkle in 1 tablespoon of the gelatin powder. Stir. Add the rest of the gelatin the same way.

2. **Add hot water and stir until well mixed.** Let sit until solid, at least one hour.

3. **Reheat the mixture in the microwave for about 5 or 10 seconds.** Stir. Repeat until it is warm and runny. Do not let the mixture foam up or boil!

4. **Pour a thin layer of the mixture onto a plate or other mold.** Let sit again until it is solid, several hours or overnight. Peel it up from the plate. Give it a tug to test how strong and stretchy your skin is!

Try This!

To keep experimenting, make additional batches, changing the amount of each ingredient. Keep track of your formulas to find out which works best.

CREATE AN
INFLATABLE ROBOT

TOOLBOX!

° robot skin from previous project
° glossy cardboard, such as a recycled cereal box
° hot glue
° craft sticks
° 60 milliliter oral syringe (or other air pump)
° plastic tubing to fit over tip of syringe, about ½ inch outside diameter and ⅛ inch inside diameter
° plastic tubing to fit inside larger tubing, about ⅛ inch outside diameter

Mold your robot skin mixture from Step 3 of the previous activity into an inflatable shape like those used to make robot grippers and crawlers! Follow the design in the pictures or create your own design.

1. Copy the designs onto smooth cardboard. "Draw" over the marks with hot glue. Make the outer lines higher than the inside lines by adding a second layer of glue.

2. Starting from Step 3 of the robot skin project, pour the mixture into the mold. Make sure the mixture covers the inside lines. Then, make a separate bottom layer by pouring a thin pool of mixture onto a flat surface, larger than the molded part. Save some extra mixture for gluing the parts together later. Let sit until dry, several hours or overnight.

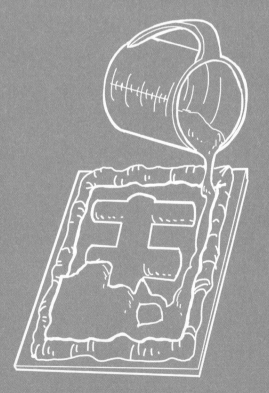

Harrison Young's Soft Robots

Harrison Young created his first homemade inflatable robots when he was in high school. As a student at Olin College of Engineering, he and his team won the 2018 Soft Robotic Design Competition with a crawling robot made from a wiggly water tube toy.

🔎 shape memory alloy

Check out his designs for a three-fingered inflatable gripper here.

🔎 Instructables grabber

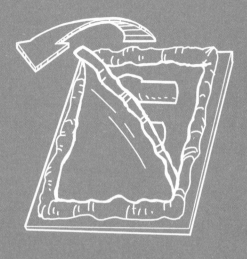

3. Carefully remove the two gripper pieces. Turn them over. To glue the pieces together, reheat the extra mixture in the microwave until runny. Use the craft stick to spread a thin layer of mixture over the flat piece.

4. On the molded piece, place the straw into the end of the air tunnel. Carefully turn the molded piece over and lay it on top of the flat piece. Press gently so the two pieces stick together. Spread more of the extra mixture around the sides to plug any holes. Let sit until solid and dry.

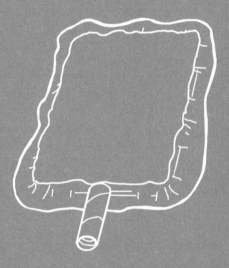

5. Remove the straw and insert a piece of thin plastic tubing. Connect it to the larger tubing, and connect that to the syringe or other air pump. Inflate your robot! If air leaks around the tubing, seal it with more gelatin mixture or press it closed with your finger.

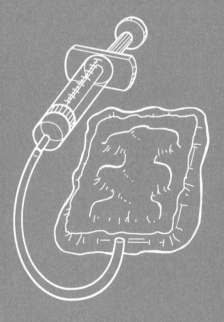

Try This!

Can you think of ways to make the inflatable robot gripper curve around an object that it is picking up? What do you need to consider?

Chapter 3

ACTUATORS:
MAKING ROBOTS MOVE

Just as with living things, robots need energy to move and "think." Even the earliest automata were powered—by humans. People raised the weights, turned the cranks, and wound up the springs that made them move. But today, we have **actuators** with batteries.

A battery is a portable power plant that uses a chemical reaction to produce **electricity**. The kinds of batteries used in robots can range in size from thin strips about half the size of a stick of gum to big, heavy car batteries the size of a cinder block.

How does electricity work? It all starts with an electric circuit.

ESSENTIAL QUESTION

How could new power sources help the development of better robots? What ideas do you have for unique ways to power robots?

HOW DOES AN ELECTRIC CIRCUIT WORK?

Atoms are extremely tiny building blocks that make up everything. The **nucleus** is the center of an atom. It contains **protons**, which have a positive (+) charge. Around the nucleus is a cloud of **electrons**, which have a negative (-) charge.

You are made of
ATOMS, your chair
is made of atoms,
AND THE APPLE
your had for breakfast
is made of atoms.

Negative particles **repel** other negative particles. They **attract**, or are pulled toward, positive particles. So, protons and electrons are pulled toward each other, while electrons push away from each other.

A battery is made up of two different metals in a container filled with acid. The acid is a chemical that allows charged particles to move around. One metal in a battery is slightly negative and the other metal is slightly positive. Electrons can move through the acid from the negatively charged metal to the positively charged metal. We call this movement electricity. The amount of electrical energy available in a battery is its **voltage**.

A circuit is a path made up of **conductive** material that allows electrons to flow. That flow is also known as electric **current**.

WORDS TO KNOW

actuator: a piece of equipment that makes a robot move.

electricity: a form of energy produced by the movement of charged particles between atoms.

atoms: the extremely tiny building blocks that make up all matter.

nucleus: the center of an atom.

proton: one of the particles that make up atoms. It carries a positive charge.

electron: one of the particles that make up atoms. It carries a negative charge.

repel: to push away.

attract: to pull toward.

voltage: the amount of electrical energy available to flow between two points in a circuit. It is measured in volts. Every electronic part in a circuit requires a certain amount of voltage to run.

conductive: describes a material that carries electricity easily. Metal is conductive, as are most wet surfaces, including skin.

current: the flow of electricity through a circuit.

WORDS TO KNOW

closed circuit: an electric circuit that provides an unbroken path for the flow of current.

open circuit: a circuit with a break in the path that prevents electricity from flowing.

solar cell: a device that converts the energy in light into electrical energy.

insulation: material that slows or prevents electricity from flowing. Plastic, rubber, and paper can be used to insulate circuits.

switch: a device that controls the flow of electricity through a circuit.

short circuit: a direct connection between two points in a circuit that aren't supposed to be directly connected.

But even when a circuit is connected to a battery, the current won't start to flow until it has somewhere to go. So, a circuit is usually connected in a loop. A **closed circuit** is when electrons can flow out of one end (or terminal) of the battery, travel around the circuit, and return back into the other end of the battery. An **open circuit** has a break or gap in the loop that prevents the electricity from flowing.

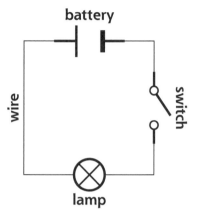

A simple diagram of a circuit powering a light

Solar Electricity

Another source of electricity for robots is the sun. That's what the early Mars rovers used. A **solar cell** uses light rays to knock electrons off of atoms and set them in motion. Solar-powered robots need some kind of storage system, such as a rechargeable battery, so they can work even when it's not light out. In 2017, Joseph Jones, who helped create the Roomba robotic vacuum, developed an autonomous, solar-powered gardening robot. The Franklin Robotics Tertill patrolled for weeds and cut them down. It could stay outside all season or even all year, rain or shine, and work on its own without human control.

To use electricity, you have to control where and when a current flows. So, a circuit is usually surrounded by **insulation** that prevents electrons from jumping off the path. A **switch** is another way to control electric flow. It opens and closes like a drawbridge. When the switch is open, no electricity can travel over the circuit. But when it is closed, the circuit is complete and the power starts humming!

A **short circuit** occurs when a piece of conductive material touches a point in a circuit that is not properly insulated or when the ends of a battery are connected to each other without something in between, such as a motor or a light. Either type can give you a shock or even cause a circuit to get dangerously hot, so be careful when making your own circuits!

Some kinds of batteries can also be plugged into **AC RECHARGERS** when they have no more charge to flow, so they can be **USED AGAIN**.

Beach Combing

Probably one of the strangest ways to power a robot is with the wind. Dutch artist Theo Jansen (1948–) builds autonomous, wind-powered walking machines called Strandbeests, or "beach animals." They consist of multiple pairs of legs made out of plastic tubes that step across the sand. Propellers or sails collect the wind, which is stored in recycled lemonade bottles in the Strandbeest's belly. When the air pressure in the bottles is released, it powers the legs. A narrow tube called a "feeler" drags along the ground and sucks in water when the Strandbeest gets too near the sea. This resets the machine's "brain" and makes it back up, toward land. The artist took simple ideas and put them together in complex ways that make his creations appear lifelike.

Take a look at his creations in action!

🔎 New Yorker wind robot

NUCLEAR POWER

Early Mars rovers that relied on solar energy had a problem—when the dust got too thick on their solar panels, they'd be stuck without power. So, NASA came up with a solution. It equipped the *Curiosity* and the *Mars 2020* rovers with **nuclear** generators. These use the enormous supply of energy released when the nucleus of an atom is split apart.

How Motors Work

Motors work by using temporary electromagnets. When electricity flows through a wire, it becomes magnetic. But unlike permanent magnets, you can turn an electromagnet off by turning off the electricity. In a motor, the shaft—the part that spins—holds several electromagnetic coils of wire. Around it is a ring of permanent magnets. All magnets have a positive side and a negative side, or pole. When you put one magnet near another magnet, their opposite poles pull toward each other, and their like poles push away from each other. Turn on a motor and the electromagnetic wire coils are pulled and pushed by the magnetic forces of the permanent magnets around them. That pull and push makes the shaft spin, and the motor turns until you shut the power off.

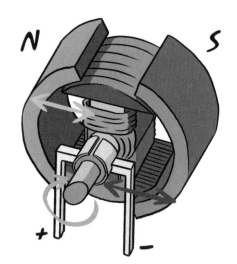

POWER SYSTEMS

No matter where it gets its power, the part of a robot that makes it move is called an actuator. Robot builders use several different kinds of actuators.

Motors are usually connected to machines by gears. Gears are wheels with interlocking teeth. They transfer the turning motion of the motor to the moving parts of the machine. Gears can also make the moving parts go faster or slower than the motor, or give them more force or **torque**.

A six-legged robot may have a **SERVO** on each leg that can be **PROGRAMMED** to make the legs move independently or all together.

Many robots use a special kind of motor called a **servo**. A servo has a feedback system that tells the robot's controller how far the shaft of the motor has turned to the right or left. A servo can be used to make a robot's arm go up to a certain point and stop. Or it can make a robot turn its head back and forth. The project on page 90 uses servos to make designs, including a crawling robot inchworm!

hydraulic: a system that pushes and pulls objects using tubes filled with fluid.

pneumatic: a system that pushes and pulls objects using tubes filled with air or other gases.

solenoid: an electromagnetic device that pushes a rod up and down.

shape memory alloy (SMA): a special combination of metals that has one shape when at one temperature but can be "trained" to remember its original shape at a different temperature.

Some robots use other types of devices to make them move. **Hydraulic** systems use the force of a fluid, such as water or oil, which is pushed through tubes by electric motors. They are very powerful, and are used by industrial robots that must lift heavy weights.

Pneumatic systems are similar, but they use air or other gases instead of fluid. They are quieter than hydraulic systems, but not as strong. Pneumatics are often used to open and close robotic grippers. Both hydraulic and pneumatic systems use a **solenoid** to push a rod up and down.

Shape memory alloy (SMA) wire, also known as muscle wire, can move robots that are soft, tiny, or made of lightweight materials such as paper and fabric. SMA wire is made of a special combination of metals. It can be trained to remember one shape when it is hot and another when it is cold. When electric current runs through it, the wire heats up. When the current is turned off, the wire cools.

Magnet Power

At Harvard in 2017, researchers used coils of SMA wire to build robots the size of a quarter that could move without batteries or motors. The robots had little hinges that could bend and miniature grippers that could open and close. The electric current was created by placing electromagnets near the SMA wire coils to get the electrons flowing.

The shrinking and stretching wire can be used **LIKE A PUPPET STRING** to pull **ROBOT PARTS** back and forth.

ACTUATORS: MAKING ROBOTS MOVE

In 2019, students at the University of Michigan created a robotic jellyfish from a rubber disk with flaps around the edge. To make the robot swim, SMA wire springs pulled the flaps in and out, just like the tentacles of the actual sea creature.

Learn more about the robotic jellyfish at this website.

robotic jellyfish SPIE 2019

PS

GETTING AROUND

Some robots, especially those in factories, are built to stay in one place and have work brought to them. Other robots travel around to where they are needed. The most common way for robots to get around is on wheels.

NASA's rovers move on wheels

credit: NASA/JPL

Some robots fly

Many hobby robots have two wheels and a support to keep them from tipping over. The support can be a smaller wheel that rolls freely without a motor, a **caster**, or simply a smooth knob that slides over the floor easily.

MicroTugs!

At Stanford University in 2010, researchers designed a robot called Stickybot that could climb up a window. It had feet like a gecko lizard that could stick to smooth surfaces but pull off easily. In 2016, Stanford students used the gecko foot design to create a microTug microrobot the size of a matchbox that could pull 2,000 times its own weight. A swarm of six microTugs was strong enough to pull a 2-ton car!

Watch a video to see the microTug in action!

🔎 microTug video

There are also two-wheeled balancing robots. These have sensors and controls that keep them shifting backward and forward so they don't lean over too far. Robots with three or four wheels can drive around like cars. For extra **stability**, some are built with more than four wheels. And rugged military robots often roll around on treads, just like tanks.

Walking on two legs may be easy for humans, but not for robots! In humans, the brain automatically adjusts our bodies every time we move to keep us from falling over. To get a robot to balance while standing, walking, running, or going up stairs takes a lot of complicated programming.

One of the most well-known walking humanoid robots is ASIMO. The Honda car company developed ASIMO in 2000 and displayed it at educational events. The Atlas robot developed by Boston Dynamics went even further. In 2017, it could hop up onto large blocks and do a backflip.

All of this power is for a purpose—to perform a task. How, exactly, do robots lift and carry objects or otherwise change the world around them? We'll take a look in the next chapter.

Atlas, 2013
credit: DARPA

ESSENTIAL QUESTION

How could new power sources help the development of better robots? What ideas do you have for unique ways to power robots?

BEAM Me Up!

Before computer chips made it easy to program robots, many hobbyists enjoyed making solar-powered BEAM robots. Their circuits were built from simple components. Instead of a battery, they stored their energy in capacitors. When the capacitor was full, it released all its energy at once, making the robot jump and move as if it were alive. Robotics physicist Mark Tilden (1961–) came up with the idea for BEAM robotics in 1989. He also designed robot toys, including Robosapien, the soccer-playing robots shown on page 14. He thought of them as primitive life forms that could **evolve** as people developed their own versions. Many BEAM robots looked like bugs or small mechanical machines. You can still buy robot kits and toys that work like BEAM robots.

SOLAR
WOBBLEBOT

This primitive robot was inspired by BEAM-style robotics. It has no "brain," but it does react unpredictably to intense light by wobbling around on its one foot!

> **SAFETY NOTE:** Have an adult help with the hot glue gun.

1. **If you are reusing a solar panel from a garden light, open the light compartment and remove any batteries or capacitors.** You will see two wires connecting the solar panel to a circuit board. Cut the wires, leaving as much wire connected to the solar panel as possible. If necessary, use a wire stripper to remove ¼ inch of the plastic insulation from the wires.

2. **Test your circuit by connecting the wires from the solar panel to the wires from the motor.** (It doesn't matter which.) Twist the metal parts of the wires together. Hold the panel up to direct sunlight or a very bright indoor light. The shaft of the motor should turn. If the motor doesn't turn, try spinning the shaft with your fingers to start it or see the Troubleshooting Tips.

3. **Hot glue the CD to the motor with the shaft sticking through the hole of the disk.** Be careful not to get any glue in the motor or on the moving parts. Add some tape if needed for extra security.

4. **Place the clear dome top over the other end of the motor.** Pull the motor wires through the hole at the top, where the straw would go. Glue the bottom of the dome onto the CD.

TOOLBOX!

- solar panel (at least 0.5 volts, or the same as your motor—you may need 2 panels if using recycled solar garden lights)
- DC motor with wires attached (0.5–2 volt "solar motors" sold by science supply retailers, or reuse a motor from a handheld fan or electric toothbrush that takes one or two 1.5 volt batteries, such as AA or AAA)
- extra insulated single-strand wire, if needed for motor
- electrical tape
- recycled CD or DVD
- recycled clear dome from drink cup or other plastic container
- aluminum foil
- high-powered shop light if direct sunshine is not available

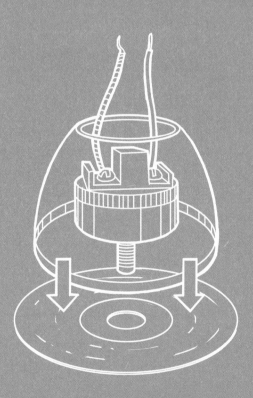

5. Twist the motor wires and the solar panel wires together again. Make sure the metal parts are touching!

6. Tear off a tiny piece of aluminum foil and squeeze it as tightly as you can around the twisted wires. This is called **crimping**, and it will help the wires stay connected as your robot jiggles around. Wrap electrical tape around the foil until there is no metal showing. Push any loose wires inside the dome. Test your circuit again to make sure you have a good connection. Then, hot glue the solar panel onto the CD, over the motor.

7. Take the Solar WobbleBot outside in bright sunlight to see how it moves. Place the bot on a very smooth, flat surface, such as a sheet of cardboard or foam core. Point the solar panel toward the sun. The motor shaft should spin and make the bot dance and skip around!

Troubleshooting Tips

› Make sure the metal part of any wires you connect are touching each other. Remember, they need to stay together even when the WobbleBot is shaking.

› If you are testing your circuit in the sun, find a spot with no shade. Clouds passing overhead may block the sun's energy, so wait for them to go by.

› If your motor turns when you hold it up but doesn't make the WobbleBot spin around, make sure the surface you are using it on isn't rough or bumpy.

› If you have tried everything and your motor won't turn, it may need more power from the solar panel. You can increase the voltage by connecting two solar garden light panels together. Hot glue them side-by-side so they both face the light at the same time. Then, twist the positive wire from one solar panel (usually white or red) together with the negative wire of the other solar panel (usually black). Connect the motor to the remaining wires as usual.

WORDS TO KNOW

crimping: connecting two pieces of metal by squishing them together.

49

PASSIVE DYNAMIC
MINI-WALKER

TOOLBOX!

- card stock
- sharp pencil
- bamboo skewer about 10 inches long
- 1 small sheet craft foam (peel-and-stick is best)
- wooden or plastic beads, about ½ inches across, with holes big enough to fit onto the skewer
- mini craft sticks about 2½ inches long
- large sheet of heavy cardboard to make a ramp
- masking tape to make walking paths (optional)

Some robotics models don't need a motor or actuator to make them move. They can use **gravity**! Roboticists call this kind of model a passive dynamic walker. Just set it at the top of a slightly downward-tilted surface and gravity will pull it the rest of the way. This method of walking doesn't just save energy, it looks more natural, too. Here is one way of making a small-scale passive dynamic walker.

1. Follow the diagram shown here to make two "L" shaped legs from card stock. Cut out two strips about 3 inches long and 1½ inches wide. From one corner of each strip, cut out a section 2 inches long and ½ inch wide. **Important:** As you build the legs, make sure they match so your walker stands evenly on its feet!

2. Use the pencil to poke a hole through the tops of the legs, near the center. Insert the skewer through the holes. Make sure the legs can swing back and forth freely. If not, make the holes bigger.

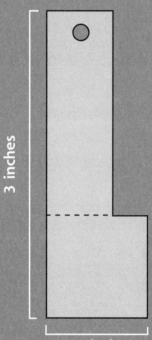

3 inches

1½ inches

Troubleshooting Tips

Check to make sure the following are true:

› The legs can swing back and forth freely

› The beads are not sliding on the skewer

› The feet have traction to grip the test ramp

› The body is balanced in the middle of the rod

WORDS TO KNOW

gravity: a force that pulls all objects toward the earth.

3. **Remove one leg, slide a bead on to the middle of the skewer,** then replace the leg on the other side of the bead. With the toes pointing toward you, fold one foot out to the left, and the other foot to the right.

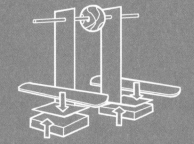

4. **Trace and cut out two pieces of craft foam the same size as the foot.**
Attach the foam to the bottom of each foot for traction. Stand the walker on its feet. Use a glue stick to attach a mini-craft stick on top of each foot, right next to the leg. The craft stick should stick out a bit more in the front, like a ski. It adds weight to help the leg swing.

5. **For the "shoulders," slide two beads onto the skewer on the outside of the legs to hold them in place.**
They should be almost touching the legs. Leave just enough room for the legs to swing back and forth freely. If the beads don't stay in place, wrap a rubber band, ziptie, or little piece of tape around the skewer to keep them from sliding around.

6. **For the "hands," stick a bead on each end of the skewer.** The weight at the ends helps the robot tip back and forth as it walks. If the beads don't stay in place, use rubber bands, zipties, or tape to hold them on.

Try This!

Experiment with different sizes and shapes, or use other materials that you have on hand. You can also try four legs instead of two, give your walker knees, or attach swinging arms to add energy to each step.

7. **Make a slanted test ramp with a piece of board.** To test the walker, set it at the top of the ramp and gently tap one end of the skewer. The walker should tip from side to side as it makes its way downhill.

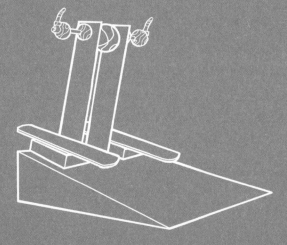

Chapter 4

HOW ROBOTS
DO THINGS

What do you use to **manipulate** the world around you? Your arms, legs, hands, and feet? Robots need parts that let them lift things, carry objects, and otherwise affect their environment—these parts are called effectors.

An effector might be an arm, gripper, tool, weapon, light, or speaker. On an industrial robot arm, an effector can be a paint gun or a **welding tool**. One kind of effector on NASA's Mars rovers *Spirit* and *Opportunity* was a tool to grind up rock samples from the planet's surface.

Robots that draw, including your ArtBot, use pens for effectors. So does the Eggbot, a programmable robot that draws detailed designs on eggshells.

ESSENTIAL QUESTION

Why is it difficult to build robotic effectors that work as well as human arms and legs?

For a household robot, an effector can be a vacuum, mower blade, or a mop. In a smart home, effectors can be overhead lights, stereo systems, and other built-in appliances with robotic controls.

A powered exoskeleton that magnifies the user's motions is another kind of effector. The ReWalk exoskeleton helps disabled people move more naturally. Other kinds of exoskeletons give a person with ordinary abilities extra strength and speed.

WORDS TO KNOW

manipulate: to handle or control.

welding tool: a blowtorch or other device that joins two pieces of metal together by heating them until they melt.

A robotic **IRON MAN SUIT** is still a way off! Early versions were too heavy and bulky. Newer **EXOSKELETONS** just move one part of the body and are lighter.

Dr. Courtney Webster works on the Warrior Web physical augmentation suit from Harvard's Wyss Institute.

credit David McNally, Army Research Laboratory

BOTS!

The *Hand Of Man*, by animatronic artist Christian Ristow (1970–), is a gigantic metal sculpture in the shape of a human arm. Kids and adults can use a control glove to make the hydraulic-powered hand pick up cars and crush them. **See a video of the artist explaining his work here.**

🔎 Christian Ristow Hand of Man

PS

DEGREES OF FREEDOM

Effectors and other parts of the robot that can move around have different **degrees of freedom**. Each direction in which a robotic part can move is one degree of freedom. An arm that can move only up and down has one degree of freedom. If it can also move side to side, it has two degrees of freedom. And if it can also rotate around in either direction, it has three.

Each degree of freedom usually needs a **joint** and an actuator to move it. The joint allows the robot part to move in one or more ways.

A robot arm with three degrees of freedom can usually reach anything within its area. Even more degrees of freedom can sometimes make it more useful.

Robots That Help Kids Walk

A robotic exoskeleton from the National Institutes of Health may someday help kids with **cerebral palsy** walk better. It only delivers bursts of support when needed. Children who tested the exoskeletons in 2017 were able to walk on their own using just the exoskeleton.

It might seem like adding more degrees of freedom would be a good thing. But each extra degree of freedom makes the robot more complicated to build. All the different movements have to be powered and controlled so they all work together. That's why many robots use simpler designs.

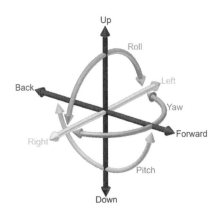

The **CANADARM 2** on the International Space Station had **SEVEN DEGREES** of freedom.

For example, some robot hands pull the fingers closed with cables that are controlled by a single motor, similar to **tendons** on a human hand.

Now we know how robots affect their environments—but how do they know where to move their effectors? They'd be lost without their sensors. We'll learn more about these in the next chapter.

ESSENTIAL QUESTION

Why is it difficult to build robotic effectors that work as well as human arms and legs?

Soft Robotic Effectors

Soft robotic arms, legs, and grippers let machines move all around without joints. A German company called Festo makes a Bionic Handling Assistant that can curl and bend like an elephant's trunk. The arm has 13 pneumatic actuators and 11 degrees of freedom. But the whole thing is made out of rings of flexible plastic, so there are no joints. At the end of the "trunk" is a three-fingered gripper. The finger design is based on the fin of a fish.

ROBOTIC HAND

TOOLBOX!

° 1 sheet of card stock or other thin, stiff cardboard
° marker
° clear tape
° 3–4 drinking straws
° 5 pieces of string, each about 10 inches long

This cardboard robotic hand works like the cable-controlled hands created by e-NABLE volunteers mentioned in the Introduction. It uses pull-strings to make the fingers open and close realistically. Test its grip by using it to lift a model car, like the giant *Hand of Man* sculpture!

1. **Using the diagram as a guide, create the pieces for your robotic hand.**

* For the palm of your robot hand, cut out a 4-inch square of cardboard.

* For the fingers, cut out four rectangles, each ¾ inch wide and 3 inches long.

* For the thumb, cut out a rectangle 1 inch wide and 2 inches long.

* Draw horizontal lines to divide each finger and the thumb into 1-inch sections. These are the joints.

2. **Lay out your robot hand as shown in the diagram.** Line up the fingers along the top of the palm and the thumb on the side.

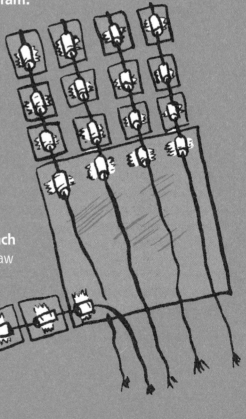

3. **Cut the fingers and thumb into sections** along the joint lines. Reassemble, leaving a little space between each section.

4. **Use tape to connect the finger sections to each other and to the palm**, making sure to keep a space between each section. Tape the front and back for extra strength.

5. **Cut the straws into 19 pieces, each about ½ inch long.** On the inside of the hand, tape one piece of straw onto each finger section and onto the palm below each finger, as shown. Trim the tape if needed, so it doesn't hang over the edge of the straw.

6. Thread one string through the straws for each finger. A crochet hook will help you pull the string through the straws. Tape the end of the string over the tip of the finger, leaving the lower end hanging loose.

7. Pull the strings to curl the fingers inward. With a little practice, you'll be able to make your robot hand point or pick up objects with amazingly lifelike gestures.

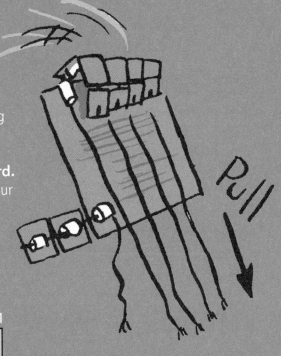

12, 1x¾ inch pieces

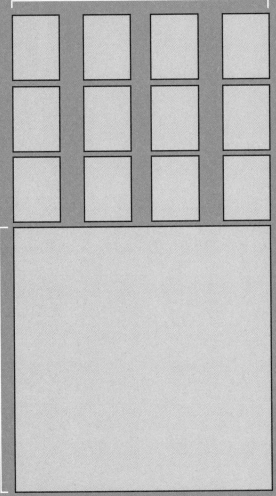

4 inches

4 inches

2, 1x1 inch pieces
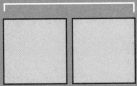

Try This!

You can extend your hand by adding a wrist or forearm. You can also adapt this design to create a robotic hand that works with the hydraulic arm in the next project!

HYDRAULIC
ROBOT ARM

This robotic arm has only two degrees of freedom but it can still bend down and pick up objects. It uses hydraulic power to move each joint.

1. Cut two long strips of cardboard for the side pieces of the arm. These should be about as wide and long as the paper towel tubes.

2. Cover all of the cardboard, including the box, with duct tape.

3. Take one of the paper towel tubes to make a tower to hold the arm. About 2 inches from one end, poke the pencil straight through the tube so it sticks out both sides. This is the bottom of the tower. Pull the pencil out. Poke another hole about 1 inch above one of the first holes, but don't go all the way through the other side. This is the back of the tower. Turn the tube so you're looking at one "side" of the tower. About 2 inches from the top, poke the pencil straight through from side to side, then remove it.

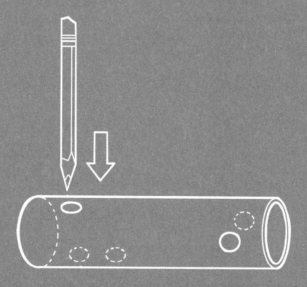

4. Cut a piece of vinyl tubing about 2 feet long. Thread it straight through the bottom set of holes so some tubing is sticking out both ends. Cut a second piece 3 feet long. Thread it into the single hole near the bottom and out through the top.

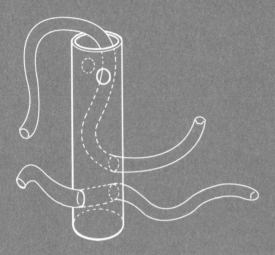

5. Lay the box flat to be the base of the arm. Tape the bottom of the tower to the base near one end with the front of the tower facing toward the nearest edge.

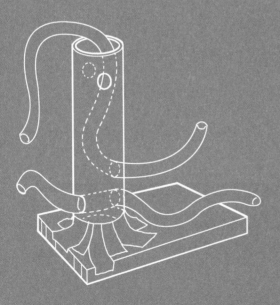

6. Hold the end of one of the side pieces over one of the holes in the top of the tower. Take the pencil and poke a hole through the side piece and through both holes in the tower. Line the other side piece up with the first and push it onto the pencil point. Leave the pencil there as a rod to hold the arm. If the point is sharp, break it off or cover it with a pencil eraser cap.

7. To make the arm, take the other paper towel tube and lay it down. Lay a syringe along the tube so the end of the plunger hangs off the end of the tube. Use clear packing tape to secure the syringe to the tube. Cover the ends of the clear tape with duct tape for a better hold, but keep the middle clear so you can watch the pump in action.

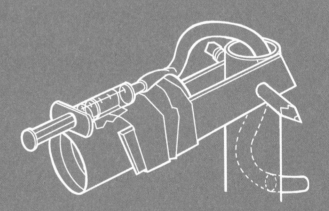

8. Position the tube between the side pieces of the arm with the plunger facing away from the tower. Move it so that the end of the plunger almost touches the table when the arm is down, but the tube doesn't hit the tower.

continued on next page . . .

9. Duct tape the tube in place between the arms. Attach the tubing coming out of the top of the tower to the tip of the syringe. Connect the other end of the same tubing to another syringe to make a hydraulic system control pump.

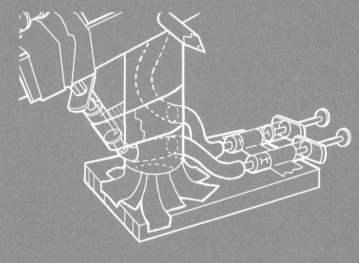

10. To move the arm up and down, connect the third syringe to the shorter piece of tubing coming out the bottom of the tower in front. Pull its plunger out almost all the way. Rest the arm on the plunger so it is sticking straight out. Use a long strip of clear tape going from the tower to the syringe and back to hold the syringe in position. The syringe should be covered by tape on both sides. Insert the remaining syringe into the other end of the tubing.

11. Before you add any water, test the systems using pneumatic power. Push in the plunger on one control pump. Make sure the plunger at the other end of the tubing slides out. If there's no rubber ring and air is leaking in, take out the plungers and try wrapping a very small rubber band or the ring from the end of a rubber balloon near the end. Replace the plungers.

RoboHands for Kids

Simple arm and leg designs used by robots can sometimes be adapted as artificial limbs for humans. And some kids are even starting to make their own! In 2015, 10-year-old Colin Consavage of Delaware made himself a cable-controlled hand using the 3-D printer at his local library. He used a design from the e-NABLE project, which also connects kids who are missing part or all of a hand with volunteers who build custom-designed **prosthetic** hands for them using 3-D printers.

Watch a video about e-NABLE hands

🔍 e-NABLE volunteers offer prosthetic hands youtube

12. To fill the tubing with water, take one syringe and pull the plunger out. Make sure the plunger at the other end of the tubing is pressed in as far as it can go. Hold the open syringe upright and fill it with water. Add a drop or two of food coloring. Then, replace the plunger and push it in all the way. Now, pick up the arm by the base and turn it so the syringe at the other end of the tubing is pointing up. Remove its plunger, and fill any remaining space with water. Replace the plunger. Slowly push the water back and forth a few times. If necessary, repeat these steps to let air bubbles escape, and add more water or food coloring. Be careful not to overfill the system or it will make the plunger pop out of the pump! When you have one system working, do the same with the other, using a different color for the water.

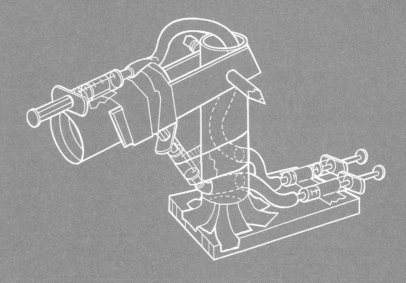

13. When everything's working, tape down the control pumps to the base. Make sure their plungers hang off the end so they can move as much as needed. Next, take a small piece of foam tape and attach it to the underside of the arm where it rests on the slanted syringe. This will help keep the arm from sliding too far out of place.

14. Finally, test your robotic arm. Find a lightweight object with a large opening, loop, or hook. See if you can make the arm bend down and pick up the object with the end plunger. It may take a little practice to push the right pump at the right time! If you want to add a gripper, do some research to find designs that can be opened and closed by moving the end plunger in and out.

Try This!

Increase the degrees of freedom by adding a swivel base that turns back and forth, another arm section that bends up and down, and a gripper that opens and closes.

WORDS TO KNOW

prosthetic: an artificial body part, such as an arm or leg.

Chapter 5

SENSORS:
WHAT IS GOING ON?

Robots, like living things, use their senses to figure out what is happening around them. For humans, those senses include seeing, hearing, touching, smelling, and tasting.

A robot's sensors work very much like ours. They take in information and convert it into an electrical signal that the robot's brain can understand. The information the sensor collects is called **input**. The robot's brain takes the input and decides what to do, based on its design or program. Then, the robot uses its effectors to respond. That response is called the robot's **output**.

A sensor for a robot can be as simple as a mechanical on-off switch. For instance, a **lever** or button on the front of a robot can act as a touch sensor. When the robot bumps into something, the lever moves. This tells the robot there's something in the way so it can change course.

ESSENTIAL QUESTION

Why do robots need so many different kinds of sensors?

OTHER TYPES OF SENSORS

A **tilt switch** is another kind of simple sensor. One version consists of a tube with a small metal ball inside. When it is tipped to one side, the metal ball rolls down to the end of the tube and touches two wires. The conductive ball bridges the gap between the wires and closes an electrical circuit. This sends a signal to the robot that indicates it is leaning over too far.

Electronic sensors work by converting an outside condition, such as temperature or light level, into electrical signals. Instead of simply turning a switch on or off, an electronic sensor can tell the robot how much of something is being detected.

An example is an **accelerometer**. This is a type of electronic tilt sensor, but it doesn't just alert the robot when it's leaning over. It also monitors how far it's leaning over and in what direction. It even detects vibrations and other movement.

An accelerometer does this by measuring how much force is pulling on it. This can be the force of gravity that pulls it toward the ground or the force felt when it moves forward or backward. Think about the pull you feel when you go up or down in an elevator or back and forth when a train starts or stops.

When you turn a smartphone sideways, an accelerometer rotates the image on the display screen around to match. GAME CONTROLLERS use accelerometers to help track the way you twist and turn them. And accelerometers activate the AIRBAGS IN CARS when they suddenly stop in a crash.

WORDS TO KNOW

input: a signal or information that is put into a machine or electrical system.

output: the movement or other response of a robot to the input it receives from its sensors.

lever: a bar or handle used to run or adjust something.

tilt switch: a sensor that turns on an electrical device when it is tilted.

accelerometer: an electronic component that uses gravity to tell how a device is tilted and how fast it is moving.

The accelerometer can turn force into electrical signals in different ways. Some versions contain a special material that produces electricity when forces squeeze it. In others, a force presses two tiny electrified conductive plates closer together or pulls them apart, which changes the electric field in the space between them.

DO YOU SEE WHAT A ROBOT SEES?

Some robots use light sensors that act as electronic eyes. They let the robot know how light or dark it is. One common type of light sensor is known as a photoresistor (*photo* means "light"). A **resistor** is an electronic component that adds **resistance** to a circuit. It makes it harder for electricity to flow.

A tiny accelerometer

credit: Simon Fraser University (CC BY 2.0)

A photoresistor is made with a chemical that has a lower resistance when light is shining on it. The more light, the more electricity flowing through the circuit. This can be used to make a robot behave differently depending on whether it's bright or shady.

Sometimes, **LEDs**—tiny, super-efficient light bulbs—are also used as light detectors. Inside an LED are materials that give off light when electricity flows through them. If you shine a light on an LED, the opposite happens— the LED converts the light's energy into electricity. This can be used to send signals to the robot's brain.

UV LIGHT is INVISIBLE to human eyes, but some insects and birds use UV light from the sky to help them figure out where they are, even when it's dark or cloudy.

Many animals have the ability to sense things humans can't. Robots have sensors that can do that, too. Have you ever seen something glow under a "black light" bulb? That glow comes from the bulb's **ultraviolet (UV)** radiation.

Using a Plant as a Light Sensor

In 2018, MIT researcher Harpreet Sareen built a robot plant called Elowan. The potted **cyborg** had a wheeled base and drove itself around in search of light. Whenever light hit the leaves, the plant sent signals to its robot brain to move in that direction. In a test, Elowan drove back and forth between two desk lamps that were turned on and off.

Read more about Elowan and watch it in action at this website.

🔍 MIT Elowan

BOTS!

Hexbot, a six-legged robot designed by French scientists in 2017, used its UV light sensors for directional help. UV light also makes certain chemicals glow. Underwater robots use UV sensors to search for oil spills, and security robots use them to hunt for explosives.

Infrared (IR) rays are also invisible to the human eye. But we can feel IR light—as heat! Some animals can "see" different temperatures the same way we see different colors. For example, rattlesnakes have IR pits near their noses that help them hunt for **warm-blooded** animals after dark.

IR LAMPS in restaurants help keep food **WARM**.

This robot has a camera, two ultrasonic sensors, and four IR sensors on its front panel.

credit: Michael Hicks (CC BY 2.0)

Robots use IR sensors to detect heat, just as rattlesnakes do. But they also use IR rays to transmit information. For example, the Lego Mindstorms EV3 robotics kit can send out an IR homing beacon that robots can follow. And swarms of more than a thousand Kilobots can be programmed at once by beaming IR light signals at the entire swarm.

I'M ON MY WAY

Along with UV light sensors, robots have lots of other ways to know where they are and what's nearby.

Ultrasonic sensors, also known as **sonar,** use sound waves too high for humans to hear to figure out how far away something is. Bats and whales use sonar to locate objects in the dark or underwater. The animals make sounds and then listen for the echo. The longer it takes for the echo to return, the farther away the object.

This self-driving car has many kinds of sensors on it.
credit Steve Jurvetson
(CC BY 2.0)

WORDS TO KNOW

proximity: how near something is.

radar: a device that detects objects by bouncing microwaves or radio waves off them and measuring how long it takes for the waves to return.

lidar: a device that measures distance by shining light at an object and measuring the time it takes for the light to reflect back.

radioactive: a substance made of atoms that gives off nuclear energy.

Many cars use **SONAR SENSORS** to warn drivers when they are **TOO CLOSE** to another car.

Hobby robots often have a pair of ultrasonic sensors mounted like eyes on the front of their "heads." The two sensors send slightly different signals to the robot's brain. They work like 3-D movie glasses—your brain combines the different images from each eye to create a picture that appears to have depth.

Robots can use other kinds of waves to measure distance. The Lego Mindstorms EV3 uses IR as a **proximity** sensor. The echo technique is also the basis of **radar**, which bounces radio waves or microwaves off an object, and **lidar**, which uses laser light waves.

Many robots are equipped with cameras and microphones, both as sensors and to act as eyes and ears for humans far away. Google's self-driving vehicle, Waymo, uses a mic as a sensor to listen for police sirens.

Where on Earth?

Robots use the same location-finding devices we do, but theirs are usually built in. A robotic compass can tell a robot the direction it's heading, similar to a compass a hiker uses. Robots also use GPS, which bounces radio waves off of satellites circling around the earth, to determine where they are on the ground.

A robot called Mini-Manbo, or "little sunfish," designed by Toshiba and an international group of researchers, was created to search a flooded Japanese nuclear power plant that was damaged by a tsunami in 2011. In 2017, Mini-Manbo sent back images of **radioactive** uranium fuel that had been missing since the original meltdown.

Mobile telepresence robots work the same way. In some cities, students who are too sick to go to school can use telepresence robots to see and hear what is going on in their classes. The robots often look like tablets mounted on a rolling stand.

In 2017, 11-year-old Cloe Gray of Maryland, who was stuck at home for months after an operation, used a telepresence made by **DOUBLE ROBOTICS** to go with her classmates to the art room, music rehearsals, or lunch.

Disney Stuntronics

Disney theme parks are famous for their animatronic characters. In 2018, the company announced it was developing acrobatic robots called Stuntronics. Advanced onboard sensors allow the machines to swing 60 feet into the air, tuck their knees, roll into a somersault, and stick a perfect landing.

Learn more about Disney's animatronics at this website.

🔎 Tech crunch Disney

Robot Whiskers

Tigers, seals, and rats use their whiskers to feel things they brush up against. Robots can use artificial whiskers as touch sensors, too. In dark or dusty conditions or underwater, whiskers work better than light sensors or cameras. They're also cheaper to replace if they break. NASA considered adding whiskers to its Mars rovers!

In 2018, an experimental "avatar cafe" employed telepresence servers controlled by disabled people from home. It allowed people who could not move to take orders, bring food to customers—and earn a salary.

All of these sensors help the robot interact with its environment. But how does a robot use information from its sensors to help it make decisions about how to act? We'll dive into robot controllers in the next chapter!

ESSENTIAL QUESTION

Why do robots need so many different kinds of sensors?

TILT
SENSOR

Make a simple tilt sensor with LED lights that indicate which way it's leaning.

1. Fold the index card in half, long edges together. On the outside, mark one side positive (+) and the other side negative (−). Unfold the card.

2. Cut four strips of aluminum foil tape that are each 2 inches long and ½ inch wide. Fold them over the long edges of the cards at the corners. Make sure the battery can touch the foil strips when it is inside the folded card.

3. Cut a strip of craft foam the same length as the card and about ¼ inch wide. Attach it to one long edge of the card.

4. Fold the card closed. Use clear tape to attach the positive (longer) lead of each LED to the foil tape pieces on the outside of the (+) side of the card. Do the same with the negative leads on the (−) side.

5. Place the battery inside the card with the (+) side facing the positive side of the card. Tape the ends closed. Then, try tilting the sensor back and forth. The LEDs should light up when the battery slides to their end.

TOOLBOX!
° index card, or thin cardboard about 3 X 5 inches
° aluminum foil tape or kitchen foil and glue stick
° peel-and-stick craft foam
° 2 LED lights
° 3V battery

Try This!

Can you improve the tilt sensor so it works better? Or, instead of LEDs, attach other small electronics such as a vibrating motor or buzzer.

PRESSURE **SENSOR**

A pressure sensor is a type of touch sensor. The harder it is pressed, the more electricity can flow through the circuit. Pressure sensors can tell a robot how tightly or gently it is holding an object in its hand, or when its foot has touched the ground. In this activity, you will use a pencil line as a pressure sensor to control an LED light. (See the box on the next page to learn how it works!) Push down lightly and the LED will be dim and flicker. Push down hard and it will glow steady and bright. Give it a try!

1. Slip the battery between the metal legs, or leads, of the LED bulb to make sure it works. The positive side (+) of the battery must face the longer lead.

2. Fold one of the shorter ends of the index card up to about the middle of the card. Unfold.

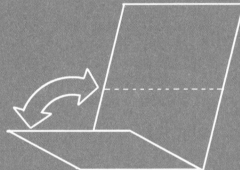

3. Cut two strips of aluminum foil tape, about ½ inch wide and long enough to reach from the other end almost to the fold. Attach the strips to the card, making sure to leave room between them for the LED. Mark the left side negative (-) and the right side positive (+).

4. Take the pencil and draw a thick, heavy stripe across the bottom edge of the card. Go over it from side to side several times. When you fold the card up, the pencil line should connect the two strips of foil and close the circuit so electricity can flow.

5. Take the battery, positive (+) side up, and place it on top of one of the foil strips as shown. The pencil line should touch the battery when the bottom flap is folded up. Use clear tape across the bottom half of the battery to secure it to the card. Make sure the pencil line can touch the uncovered part of the battery.

6. Hold the LED with the positive side (the longer lead) facing right. Carefully bend both leads out to the sides. Use clear tape to attach the positive lead to the right strip of foil and the negative lead to the left strip of foil. Make sure they make good connections.

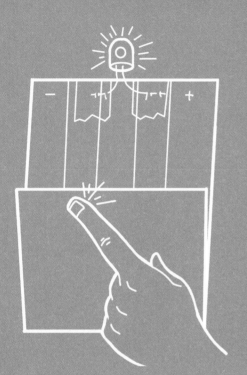

7. Fold the bottom of the card back up. Now, test the pressure sensor by pressing on the folded flap. If the LED lights up, you can tape the sides of the flap closed. Try using different amounts of pressure to make the LED brighter or dimmer. If it doesn't light up, check that all your connections are good and that the LED and battery are connected the right way.

Consider This!

Can you add a pencil-and-paper pressure sensor to one of the robot projects in this book?

Robotic Pencils

An ordinary pencil has interesting properties that scientists are hoping to use in robotics. A pencil "lead" is a mixture of graphite, which is a conductive material, and clay, which is non-conductive. That means a pencil line can carry different amounts of electricity at different times. In 2018, Australian researchers created a prototype pressure sensor with paper and pencil that allowed more electricity to flow when it was squeezed. They attached the sensor to a robot's hand and used it to measure how hard the robot squeezed a rubber ball.

See graphite in action in this video on making a closed circuit with a pencil!

🔎 Household Hacker paper circuit

Chapter 6

CONTROLLERS:
HOW ROBOTS THINK

Even a simple robot without electronics can move around in a lifelike way. But to make decisions on its own, a robot needs a "brain." A robot's computer or electronic controller takes in data from its sensors and uses that information to decide what action to take. That's how a robot thinks!

The first computers—including those built into robots—were made with **vacuum tubes**. These were electronic switches that looked like tall, thin light bulbs. Vacuum tubes took up a lot of space and could get very hot. Early vacuum tube computers might fill an entire room, but were less powerful than a smartphone is today!

ESSENTIAL QUESTION

How is a computer program for a robot different from a step-by-step set of instructions?

The invention of the **transistor** in 1947 made modern computers and robots possible. A transistor is a switch made from an **element** such as silicon that acts as a **semiconductor**. It is much easier to use than a vacuum tube and much less breakable.

Today, millions of transistors can be printed onto small squares of silicon known as **microprocessors** or **computer chips**. Developed in 1958, microprocessors are the most important part of a computer. They are so cheap and portable that they are found in almost every kind of electronic device, from toys to cars to televisions. In a microprocessor, all the transistors and other components are miniaturized, wired together, and squeezed onto a thin square the size of your fingernail.

With such **A TINY DISTANCE** between components, **ELECTRIC CURRENTS** can open and close the transistor "switches" incredibly fast.

BOTS!

WORDS TO KNOW

Wi-Fi: technology that allows the wireless transmission of radio waves.

Bluetooth: the short-range wireless interconnection of mobile phones, computers, and other electronic devices.

memory: the part of a computer where information is stored.

Tiny Companion

The Cozmo robot was a cute mini bulldozer with an animated face that could play games, talk, and even recognize family members and pets. While it had a small built-in computer to control its movements, all the heavy thinking was done by your smartphone or tablet using a special app over Wi-Fi. Cozmo was one of the best-selling toy robots until its parent company, Anki, went out of business in 2019.

As scientists figured out how to pack more computing power onto smaller and smaller chips, it became possible to give a robot its own computer. Most robots now contain some type of onboard computer.

But scientists are constantly on the lookout for new technologies they can use to make their robots smarter, faster, and way more cool. One way is to connect robots to outside computers and devices, using wireless signals such as **Wi-Fi** and **Bluetooth**.

The ENIAC computer, early 1950s

MICROCONTROLLER BRAINS

A microcontroller is a small, simple computer. It can range from tinier than a postage stamp to the size of a playing card. Built into the microcontroller are a microprocessor, input and output devices such as light sensors or speakers, **memory**, and other parts. A microcontroller can be programmed, but it has only enough memory to hold a few instructions. Even so, a microcontroller makes a great brain for a beginner-level robot. It can be used to make a robot behave in very complicated ways!

The Arduino microcontroller board was developed for college students in Italy and released to the public in 2008. It is popular with people who want to make quick **PROTOTYPES**. Since it is open source, many other **MICROCONTROLLERS** are based on its design.

PROGRAM IT!

Computers are incredibly powerful. They are very good at solving simple problems that can be expressed mathematically, such as whether one number is bigger or smaller than another. They are also amazingly quick. They can solve billions of little problems every second. However, they need a human to figure out how to take those little problems and put them together in useful ways.

The Micro:bit

In 2016, the BBC broadcasting service gave a free Micro:bit microcontroller to every year 7 student (ages 11 and 12) in the United Kingdom to help them learn to code. It's now used by students all around the world. With a built-in accelerometer, light sensor, Bluetooth, and a grid of red LEDs, it can be used to program simple robots. (Find out how later in this chapter!)

BOTS!

To decide what a robot should do next based on input from a sensor, a computer takes the numbers produced by the sensor and compares them to other numbers. Then, it follows the steps a human being programmed into it. The steps tell it what to do, depending on whether the numbers are high or low. The directions containing those steps is the computer program, also known as code or software.

A person who writes code is called a **CODER, PROGRAMMER,** or **SOFTWARE ENGINEER.**

The most important part of writing a program is breaking down everything you want the computer to do into simple steps. Leave out a step, and the computer will get stuck or do the wrong thing. One way to keep track of all the steps in a program is to start off by making a flowchart. Remember the "Robot . . . or Not?" flowchart at the beginning of this book?

Suppose you want to program a robot to follow a light. Your flowchart would have a decision block that says, "Is there light up ahead?" If the answer is "True," the program tells the robot to keep moving forward. If the answer is "False," it tells the robot to turn. In a program, you would write something like, "IF there is light ahead, THEN keep moving forward, or ELSE turn around."

This is called a **conditional statement**. Its outcome depends on whether or not a certain condition exists—in this case, whether or not there is light up ahead. It's also known as an if-then-else statement.

Conditional statements are examples of **Boolean logic**. Since a computer can only understand "on" and "off," every decision has to be a question with a true/false answer. The answer can then be translated into binary code: "on" or "off," one or zero.

Logo is a computer language developed to teach kids how to code. There are online Logo programs you can try for free. **To learn more, go to this website.**

🔍 MIT Logo

PS

Inside the computer, this is done using an electronic circuit with a **logic gate** that takes one or more input signals, analyzes them, and produces an output signal. The most common logic gates are "NOT" (the condition is not true), "AND" (there are two conditions and both are true), and "OR" (there are two conditions and at least one of them is true).

Even the most complicated computer programs can be written using these **THREE LOGIC GATES** and their variations!

Programmers have tricks they use to save space and make their code easier to understand. One shortcut is a **function**, which is a small series of commands. Instead of writing the same steps again and again, a programmer can simply write the name of the function wherever those steps are needed.

pseudocode: a computer program written out in human words instead of special programming terms (*pseudo* means "fake").

loop: a short piece of code that is repeated a certain number of times until a specific condition is met.

binary system: a math system containing only zeroes and ones. It is used by computers to indicate whether a switch is on or off.

```
Call Function [Blink]
Forward 10
Light on 1 second
Light off
End
```

An example of a function called "Blink" that tells a robot to move ahead 10 squares and then flash its light for 1 second might look like this. It is written in **pseudocode**—another way to plan a program by using everyday words instead of special computer terms.

A **loop** repeats a command or series of commands until you tell it to stop. You can do this by specifying the number of times you want it to repeat. Or you can add a conditional statement. For instance, if you wanted to program a robotic arm to move all the jelly beans from a bowl to a cup and then stop, you could write a loop like this:

```
WHILE there are jelly beans in the bowl
Pick up 1 jelly bean
Put the jelly bean in a cup
END WHILE
```

This loop uses a "WHILE" conditional statement. A while loop causes the code to repeat over and over as long as the condition is true. As soon as the condition is *not* true, the loop stops so the program can go on to the next step. As long as there is at least one jelly bean in the bowl, the computer will keep going back to the beginning of the loop and doing it all over again. When the number of jelly beans goes down to zero, the loop ends.

In the game LightBot, players program a robot to follow a path. As levels get harder, you can create functions and loops to fit in all the commands needed. LightBot has a free Hour of Code demo. **Play it online or download the app at this link.**

🔎 LightBot

COMPUTER LANGUAGES

A computer is made up of millions of switches that are either on or off. Since there are two choices, this is called the **binary system**. *Bi* is latin for "two," as in bicycle. Computer code is mathematical. If a switch is off, it's represented by zero. If it's on, it's represented by one. To a computer, a program looks like a long line of zeroes and ones.

Would you be able to understand a computer program written in binary? Probably not! Since people think in words and computers think in binary code, we need special computer languages to communicate with a robot's brain.

Some popular computer languages include **C#**, **JAVA**, and **PYTHON**.

Programming languages use text commands that are similar to English. However, if you don't get all the spelling and punctuation exactly right, the computer may not know what you're trying to say. That's why many programming languages for beginners sometimes use blocks or symbols instead of words. All you do is drag and drop the block on the computer screen. The blocks snap together like puzzle pieces. Instead of having to type in all the commands, you just find the blocks you need and line or stack them up.

BOTS!

bug: a mistake in a computer program.

debug: going through a computer program to find and remove any mistakes.

turtle robot: a robot used to teach coding using simple instructions that tell it how to move around a grid.

virtual robot: a programmable animation on a computer screen.

hardware: the body, motors, and other physical parts of a robot or other device.

If your computer program doesn't work right, it may have a **bug** in it. A bug is a mistake in the code, and to fix it you have to **"debug"** IT.

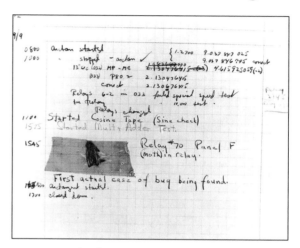

The first computer bug, 1947

The free online block-based program Scratch was developed for kids by MIT computer scientist Mitch Resnick in 2007. Its open source design inspired many other languages, such as Blockly and MakeCode. Some robotics kits and models have their own visual programming languages as well.

In 2018, Scratch 3.0 was released. It can be used with some microcontrollers and robotics kits.

Hour of Code is a worldwide event organized by a Code.org. It happens every year during Computer Science Education Week in December. But you can sample many different computer languages on the Hour of Code website anytime—for free! **Check it out at this website.**

🔎 Hour of Code

PS

Turtle Robots and Logo Programming

A **turtle robot** is a small, simple robot used to learn about robot control. Low and round or triangle-shaped, they look like turtles as they roll slowly along the floor. In the 1940s, when computers were still new, a scientist in England named William Grey Walter (1910–1977) built some of the earliest turtle robots using vacuum tubes. The robots could explore their environment with light and touch sensors. Today, turtle robots usually have a pen that traces their movement. In 1967, mathematician Seymour Papert (1928–2016) of MIT created a language called Logo to teach kids how to program by steering a **virtual robot** around the computer screen.

Programming a robot can be harder than programming a computer because you have to make sure the software works with the **hardware**! If there's a problem, you may need to adjust the code to match the sensors or the motors. Other times, it's best to change the design of the body or the wheels. Figuring out the best combination of programming and machinery is part of the fun of robotics!

ESSENTIAL QUESTION

How is a computer program for a robot different from a step-by-step set of instructions?

WRITE A
PENCIL-AND-PAPER LOGO PROGRAM

TOOLBOX!
° several sheets of graph paper
° pencils
° several sheets of lined paper
° a friend (optional)

You can practice writing code for a turtle robot even if you don't have a computer! Real programmers sometimes type code into a text document first. Then, they copy and paste it into the software to see if it works. In this activity, you will test the sample code by drawing the turtle's path on a piece of graph paper. Write your own code to make new designs!

Command	Stands for	How it Works
FD x	Forward	Replace "x" with the number of steps.
BK x	Back	Replace "x" with the number of steps
RT	Right Turn	Turn but stay on the same box.
LT	Left Turn	Turn but stay on the same box.
PU	Pen Up	Stop drawing as you move.
PD	Pen Down	Start drawing as you move.
REPEAT y [commands]	Repeat	Do the commands in the brackets. Replace "y" with the number of times to repeat them. (This is a loop.)

1. Turn the paper sideways, so it is wider than it is high. Each box on the graph paper will count as 10 steps, or pixels. That will make it come out about the same size as on a computer screen.

2. To start, place your pen near the bottom left corner of your graph paper and mark your robot's starting place. You will begin with the turtle pointing up.

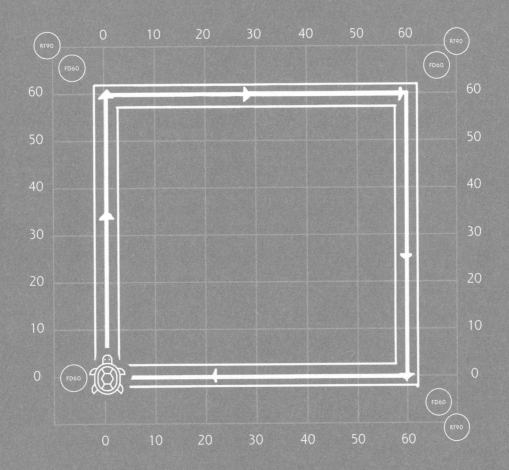

3. **Follow the commands to move your pen the same way the Logo turtle would move.** The example below will draw a square. You can have a friend read the commands to you.

PD
FD 60
RT 90
FD 60
RT 90
FD 60
RT 90
FD 60
RT 90

* **A shorter way to write the same program is to use a loop:**

REPEAT 4 [FD 60, RT 90]

Try This!

Figure out the Logo code to make a word, a name, or a design such as a smiley face. Or write out a secret message or drawing in Logo code and give it to a friend to solve.

PROGRAM A VIRTUAL
MUSICAL ROBOT
WITH SCRATCH

TOOLBOX!
° computer, tablet, or smartphone with access to Scratch 3.0

In Scratch, you can use code blocks to make an animated character move around the screen. There are even color sensor blocks you can use to program a virtual robot! In this project, you will create a cartoon robot that plays different musical notes as it drives around a path made up of different color blocks. See an example at this website.

Virtual Color-Sensing Musical Robot

1. **Open Scratch and click "Create" to start a new program.** On the stage, you'll see the Scratch Cat. This is a sprite, a movable character or object that you can program. The backdrop, which changes the look of the stage, is blank. To add, edit, or create a sprite or backdrop, mouse over the button in its section. It will let you go to a library with pre-made choices or open a new section with onscreen drawing tools.

2. **To keep track of where a sprite is on the stage,** Scratch uses an invisible grid of squares. Each square can be identified by two numbers, known as the **x and y coordinates.** Go to the backdrop library and add the *Xy-grid* to your backdrops. You won't need this backdrop for your final program, but it may be useful to look at while you're working.

Musical Color Chaser Robots

The Virtual Color-Sensing Musical Robot was inspired by artist Yuri Suzuki's tiny robotic Colour Chasers. To make the bots play different sounds, you draw a black path with a marker and scribble over it in spots with different colors.

Watch a video of the Colour Chasers at this website.

Suzuki Colour Chasers

WORDS TO KNOW

x and y coordinates: two numbers that give the position of a point on a grid of squares, where x is the horizontal distance (right or left) and y is the vertical distance (up or down) from a central point that is labeled zero.

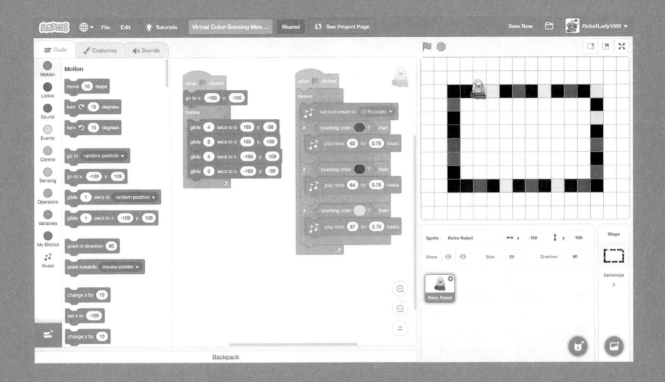

3. **To draw a path for your robot to drive around, follow these steps.**

   ✱ Go to the backdrop library and add a blank grid, such as Xy-grid-30px.

   ✱ Click on the "Backdrop" tab at the top of your editing screen to edit it.

   ✱ In "Fill," select black. Click on the paint can **icon**. Then click on each square you want to fill with color until your path is a big rectangle.

   ✱ Next, go over a few squares with two or three different colors. These will trigger the robot to play sounds.

4. **Now, click the "Code" tab to program your sprite. First, tell the robot where to start.**

   ✱ On the stage, drag the robot to the bottom left corner of the path.

   ✱ From the tan "Event" category, get a *when flag clicked* block.

   ✱ In the blue "Motion" category, find the *go to x ( ) y ( )* block. The numbers in the spaces are the coordinates for the sprite's current position. Add it underneath the flag block.

continued on next page . . .

WORDS TO KNOW

icon: a small picture that opens a tool, page, or file on a computer.

5. Then, make the robot move around the path.

* Drag the robot to the next corner. Find the *glide ()* secs block with the sprite's coordinates and drag it into the workspace. (Don't add it to the other blocks just yet.)

* Add three more glide blocks the same way until you're back at the first corner.

* From the light-orange "Control" category, get a *forever* block. Drag it around the stack of glide blocks. Drag that stack under the first stack until they connect.

* Change the number of seconds on the glide blocks to make the robot move slower.

6. Next, start a separate stack of blocks to add sensors to your robot.

* From "Control," get an *If <> then* block.

* In light-blue "Sensing," find the *touching color ()?* block. Drag the *touching color* block over the same-shaped spot in the *if <> then* block until it snaps into it.

* To set the color spot on the block, click on it to open up the color menu. At the bottom of the menu, click on the icon of an eyedropper. Mouse over a color on the path and click on it. The color on the block will change to match it.

* Duplicate the *if-then* block and make a copy for each of the colors on the path. Put the stack inside a *forever* block, so the program will be constantly checking for those colors.

Circuit Playground Express

Designed by MIT-trained engineer Limor Fried's company Adafruit, the Circuit Playground Express (CPX) is similar to the Micro:bit, but with more inputs and outputs. It has an accelerometer, a light sensor that also works as a color sensor, a sound sensor, a temperature sensor, and IR remote control and signaling. Its ring of red-green-blue (RGB) LEDs can be programmed to dim, brighten, and change color. It also has a speaker to play electronic-sounding music.

Learn more at this website.

🔍 Adafruit

7. Finally, it's time to add music blocks to your project.

✳ At the bottom of the list of categories, click the blue *Extension link*. Click "Music" to add it to the list.

✳ Drag a *play note* or *play drum* block into all the *if-then* blocks in your program. You can change which note is playing and how many beats long it plays. You can also add a block to change the instrument.

✳ Add a *when flag clicked* block from the "Event" category on top so this stack runs at the same time as the first stack. Try your program to see how it runs!

Try this!

See what happens when you change the size of the sprite, its speed, or how long the note sounds. Explore the Scratch site to find more fun programming examples.

Scratch Tips

› If you are new to Scratch, use the animated tutorials to help you get started.

› Scratch gives you a list of block categories to choose from, a workspace to put your code together, and a stage where you can see your program run.

› To test your code as you go along, click on any block or stack of blocks to make it run.

› Any character or object can have more than one stack of blocks. Use an "Event" block on each stack to tell it when to start.

› To detach blocks from a stack, pull them away from the bottom.

› To delete a block, right-click on it or drag it to the left side of the screen and it will disappear.

› To save time or to make different versions, you can click "duplicate" to make a copy of your code, characters, backdrops, or the entire program.

› To save or share your program online, create a free account. (The site is moderated, so it's safe for kids to use at school or at home.) Your program can be downloaded to your computer as well.

BUILD AND PROGRAM A
RECYCLED ROBOT WITH MAKECODE

With microcontrollers such as the Micro:bit and the Circuit Playground Express, you can build a programmable robot out of almost anything in your recycling bin! This project will show you how to connect a servo motor to one of the microcontrollers and how to program the on-board sensors with the free, online, drag-and-drop language MakeCode. You will code them to make the servo move when the board is in the shade and stop when it is brighter. What you build with them is up to you!

1. **To start, go to the MakeCode.com page and select the board you are using.** Click on "New Project." If you are using an app for your board, select "Create Project" and "Let's Code" in MakeCode.

Don't have a computer? Check to see if there's an app that lets you program your board with your mobile device over Bluetooth. Don't have a board? MakeCode's simulator runs on most computers and devices and lets you see how your code would run. The Micro:bit version also shows the servo motor.

See the completed code for this project at the links shown here.

🔎 Circuit Playground

🔎 Micro:bit

TOOLBOX!

- computer, tablet, or smartphone with internet access
- Micro:bit or Circuit Playground Express microcontroller board, often sold along with robotics kits and parts, or online at sites including:
  - adafruit.com
  - sparkfun.com
  - techwillsaveus.com
- USB data cable and/or battery case that fits your board
- alligator clip to male header test wires
- 9g micro servo motor

For head-turning robot:
- glue dots or Velcro dots
- 2 small cardboard boxes
- scissors or a craft knife
- markers
- googly eyes

2. Begin to create the code for the light sensor.

* From "Input," get the oval block near the bottom that says *light level*. Right-click to duplicate it, so you have two copies.

* Get a *graph* block to display the light level using the on-board LEDs. For the Micro:bit, it is in the "LED" category. For the CPX, find it under "Light," then click on the plus sign on the block to open another zero. Drag one of the *light level* blocks over the first zero. In the second, type 255 (the upper limit of the light sensor).

* Insert the *graph* block into the *forever* block. The simulation should start to run, showing half the LEDs lit up. To change the light level on the simulation, click on the circle near the board and drag the yellow filling up and down. The number of LEDs lit up should go up and down, too.

* Next, from "Logic," get an *if <true> then* block. Also get a *(0) < (0)* comparison block. (The arrow pointing left means "less than.") Drag the remaining *light level* block over the first zero in the comparison block until it snaps in. Type 150 over the second zero. (You may need to adjust the number when you test the real board under real lighting conditions.)

* Drag the comparison block over the pointy "true" space on the *if-then* block until it snaps in. Then, drag the entire thing inside the *forever* block.

3. Next, click on "Advanced," then on the "Extensions" link to add the "Servo" category to the list. To make the servo move back and forth, do the following steps.

* Drag a *set servo [ ] angle to (90)* block inside the *if-then* block. (The "A1" or "P0" after the servo tells you which pin, or numbered hole on the board, controls the servo.) Click on "90" to open a slider. It shows the position of the servo arm. Slide it to the left and stop at about 10 degrees.

* Duplicate the first *servo* block. Set it to about 170 degrees and attach it underneath. Then, add a third *servo* block to move the servo back to 10 degrees.

* Now, insert *pause* blocks between the *servo* blocks. For Micro:bit, *pause* is under "Basic." For CPX, it is under "Loops." Set the pauses for 1 second (1000 ms, or milliseconds). This gives the servo time to move back and forth.

* For the Micro:bit, the servo in the simulation should now be swinging.

continued on next page . . .

4. **Hook up the servo to the board.**

* Choose one of the servo arms (also known as horns) and press it onto the shaft of the motor. Adjust the way it's facing if you need to.

* The servo has three wires and a three-pin plug. To connect it to the board, take the alligator clip wires and insert the wires into the servo's plug. Try to match the colors.

5. **Connect the alligator clips** to the microcontroller pins as follows. The colors refer to the servo wires. This step is important to follow correctly so you don't damage the electronics.

* Red (power)—3V (volts) or VOUT (voltage out)

* Black/Brown (ground)—GND

* Orange/Yellow (control)—On the CPX, use Pin A1. On the Micro:bit, use Pin 0.

6. **Now, name your program!** This will help you find it later. You can save it by downloading to your computer or device. Also, click "Share" to save it on the web. Copy the webpage address for your project so you can go back to it later from any device.

7. **To download and run your program on your board, select "Download" on the MakeCode page or Flash on your board's app.** Follow the instructions or click "Help" if you have problems. Then look for your program's name in your computer's files or on the app. Move the file to the device on the computer, or click the "Play" icon on the app. If the servo arm swings back and forth, you're done! If not, shade the light sensor on the board with your hand. Or go back into the code and use a lower number for the light level.

* Connect the board to your computer with the USB cable.

* Click "Download" and follow the instructions. (For the CPX only, press the reset button once or twice to make the LEDs turn red briefly, then green.)

* Find your program's name in your computer's files. Drag or copy and paste the file to the board. It will show up as an external drive, like a flash drive. (The name of the CPX drive is CPLAYBOOT.)

* If the servo arm swings back and forth, you're done! If it doesn't, try shading the light sensor on the board with your hand. Or change the light level in the code until it works. (In a dark room, it may go as low as 10.)

8. Ready to build a cardboard robot? This quick design turns its head when someone blocks the light.

* For the head, attach a small box to the servo arm with glue dots. Add googly eyes or draw on a face.

* On a slightly larger box, make a hole on top for the servo. Also cut a small hole in the side of the box.

* Insert the servo into the top hole so the wires hang down inside the box. Bring the wires out through the hole in the side.

Try This!

For more ideas, check out the projects on the MakeCode page. For the Micro:bit, you can also go to Microbit.org. For the CPX, go to MakeCode.com. If you're interested in trying text languages, you can also program both boards in Javascript, Arduino, and Python.

🔍 MakeCode Adafruit

🔍 learn Adafruit

* If the alligator clips are not attached, connect them to the board as in Step 3.

* Use glue dots or Velcro dots to attach the microcontroller to the front of the box.

* If using batteries, glue or Velcro the battery pack to the larger box or make a slot to insert the belt clip. Disconnect the USB cable and plug in the battery pack.

* Pull any extra wire inside the box and close it up. To test your robot, wave your hand over the light sensor to make the head swivel!

Troubleshooting Tips

› MakeCode is based on Scratch, so check the Scratch Tips in the previous project for help getting started with block-based coding.

› Use the tutorials on the MakeCode pages or the "Help" button if needed.

› Be sure to give your program a name and save it online or on your computer so you can re-use and share it. If you make changes to a version you have saved online, you will have to save it again.

› Wait a few seconds for the code to load when testing it.

› If your code isn't working on your board or servo, check that the wires are attached correctly. Low batteries may also affect how well the code runs, even if the board still lights up.

Chapter 7

AI AND
THE FUTURE
OF ROBOTICS

WE DON'T KNOW WHAT THE FUTURE OF ROBOTS LOOKS LIKE.

THEY MIGHT BECOME EVEN MORE DIFFERENT FROM US...

...OR EVEN MORE SIMILAR!

It's one thing to program a robot to "think." But getting it to think like a human? That's a goal scientists have been working on since computers were developed. And it's closer than ever before.

The science of AI is all about figuring out how to make computers smarter so they don't need people to tell them what to do. Thanks to AI, robots can answer our questions, find their way around town, and even learn how to program themselves.

ESSENTIAL QUESTION

How might robots change the way we live in the future?

Early on, scientists tried to make computers act human without really changing the way they think. In 1966, Joseph Weizenbaum (1923–2008) of MIT designed Eliza, a computer program that behaved as a therapist. The program started every conversation with, "Hi, I'm Eliza. What's your problem?"

When you typed in an answer, she would respond with a related sentence, such as, "Tell me more." Although it was a very simple program, Eliza seemed to pass the Turing test. People talked to it as if it were a real person. Today, these kinds of programs are called **chatbots**.

Digital assistants such as Alexa and Siri, also known as smart speakers, are chatbots that can learn. The more you use them, the more information they gather about you. That helps them figure out what you like and what kinds of suggestions you are looking for. When you ask your digital assistant to play music, it already knows your favorite songs.

Create a Chatbot in Scratch

You can write a simple chatbot program in Scratch that asks a person questions and uses their answers to keep the conversation going.

To get started, try the chatbot tutorial on the Code Club, run by the Raspberry Pi Foundation.

🔎 Code Club chatbot

WORDS TO KNOW

natural language processing: a branch of AI that helps computers understand and use human language.

machine learning (ML): a form of AI that lets you train a computer to look for clues to the meanings of words and images. The ML program you create to analyze specific data is called a machine learning engine.

They're also getting better at sounding human. In 2018, Google introduced Duplex, a chatbot that uses **natural language processing** to talk to humans on the phone. To sound less like a robot, it added "um" and "mm-hmm" to its speech, just as people do when they need a moment to think.

Challenging a computer to a game is another way to test how smart it really is. In 1989, World Chess Champion Garry Kasparov (1963–) played two games against an IBM computer called Deep Thought. He defeated the computer both times. But in 1997, an improved version called Deep Blue played against Kasparov and won!

As it turned out, chess is easy for computers to master. They can check all possible moves to find the best one in the blink of an eye.

It's much harder **TO TEACH** a computer to play a TV game show such as **JEOPARDY!**

In 2011, people across the country watched as an IBM computer named Watson beat *Jeopardy* champion Ken Jennings (1947–). To win, players must know about a wide range of subjects. But the IBM team led by researcher David Ferrucci did more than fill Watson's memory banks with information. They taught Watson how to understand the clues, which often contain tricky wording and jokes. In the final round, Jennings didn't know the answer. Instead, he saluted Watson's ability by writing, "I for one welcome our new computer overlords."

Paul Hudson (CC BY 2.0)

MACHINE LEARNING

The AI tool that helps Watson and Siri get smarter as time goes by is known as **machine learning (ML)**. ML lets you train a computer to look for clues to the meanings of words and images by giving it examples of what you're looking for. The computer then tests new information against what it already knows. For example, if you give the computer lots of images of dogs, it will learn to find a dog in pictures by looking for four legs and a tail. To improve its accuracy, you have to give it more examples of different dogs from different perspectives.

Make Your Own ML Engine

You can find websites that let you play around with ML for free, such as IBM's Watson and Google's TensorFlow. Here are a few.

Machine Learning for Kids is a website that lets you train your own engine using IBM's Watson. Then, it creates special coding blocks you can use to make an AI program in Scratch.

🔎 Machine Learning for Kids

Cognimates teaches kids how to build games, program robots, and train their own AI models. It works with Cozmo, Micro:bit, and Scratch. (If the site doesn't work on your phone or tablet, type in the website address on a desktop or laptop computer.)

🔎 MIT Cognimates

Teachable Machine uses your webcam to record images for three different categories. You can make each category cause your computer to respond by showing a different animated gif.

🔎 Teachable Machine

PS

deep learning: an area of machine learning that uses large amounts of data and finds ways to connect them.

cloud robotics: designing robots that require computing power or information from the internet to function.

An advanced kind of ML called **deep learning** allows a computer to process larger amounts of data and compare them in more ways. It can find complicated patterns and improve its own accuracy. A deep learning machine can figure out by itself how to tell an image of a dog from a cat by picking out smaller differences in their faces and tails.

CLOUD ROBOTICS

Want to build a robot with the brain power of Watson? All you need is an internet connection. **Cloud robotics** lets any machine draw on computing power anywhere in the world. It's how self-driving cars access maps, weather reports, and up-to-the-minute traffic conditions. It also connects robots with other robots and lets robots communicate with human controllers.

A Cyborg Future?

In 2008, British engineer Kevin Warwick (1954–) used a clump of rat brain cells in a lab to control a robot over Bluetooth. The robot's living brain learned to drive around without hitting anything. Warwick—sometimes known as "Captain Cyborg"—is himself part electronic. A computer chip in his arm lets him signal his feelings to his wife using a special color-changing necklace.

Watch a TEDx talk where Kevin Warwick predicts, "In the future you will all be cyborgs . . . we will all be able to communicate just by thinking to each other."

🔎 Kevin Warwick TEDx

Cloud robotics has been used in toys such as Anki's Vector. Like its cousin Cozmo, Vector was shaped like a small and perky bulldozer. But instead of using your smartphone as its brain, Vector had the same computing power built in. Vector could show you the weather, find answers to math problems, and give you news about your favorite celebrities. It also connected with Amazon's Alexa to control lights and appliances in your home.

SOCIAL ROBOTS

Many researchers believe that **PEOPLE** get along better with **ROBOTS** that show feelings.

Even thinking like a human isn't enough for some scientists. They'd like to develop robots with personalities! Social robots are designed to work and play with people. A social robot can be friendly, even lovable.

In 1998, Cynthia Breazeal (1967–) of MIT built one of the first social robots, Kismet. It consisted of a motorized face with large eyes, soft lips, and rotating ears. When you talked to Kismet, it would respond to your tone of voice. If you spoke sharply, it would look sad. If your voice was soothing or cheerful, it would smile.

Her next robot, Leonardo, was a big-eared, fuzzy creature designed by Hollywood special effects whiz Stan Winston (1946–2008). It showed emotion with its tiny hands and body as well as its face. More recently, her team developed Tega, a furry, bouncy robot with a smartphone face designed to help young children learn.

TEGA can mirror a child's expression to **BUILD FRIENDSHIP** and **TRUST**.

Robots also use social skills to help them learn—by getting humans to help them. At the Georgia Institute of Technology, roboticist Andrea Thomaz developed humanoid robots named Simon and Curi. They learned by watching people do a task, such as sorting toys or scooping spaghetti into a bowl, and then copying them. If the robots didn't understand, they could ask questions and get people to explain things to them.

These NAO robots are the older cousins of Pepper (see Page 2). They talk and move in lifelike ways. Researchers have used NAO robots to work with autistic children, as therapists, and in nursing homes. One study found they didn't work as well as soft and cuddly therapy robots.

credit: Salford University (CC BY 2.0)

ROBOTS VERSUS HUMANS?

Robots are designed to help people live better lives. But are they really our friends?

That's the kind of question psychologist Sherry Turkle (1948–) of MIT wants people to ask themselves. She studies the ways technology affects people's lives, and one thing that concerns her is the way social robots are programmed to act as though they like us. What if a child thought a broken robot was mad at them? It can be easy to forget that robots don't really have feelings.

Some experts are afraid that people might become used to **ORDERING ROBOTS** around and **FORGET** how to **BE KIND** to living things.

A Lego Mindstorms Emotional Robot

It used to be that even small robots were expensive. Today, you can build advanced robots from low-cost materials. In 2017, a student at Queen Mary University of London built a robotic face called Blade using a Lego Mindstorms kit. He programmed Blade using AI to react to a person's tone of voice, just like the robot Kismet. When the project was done, he simply took his Lego social robot apart to use again.

Watch a video of Blade at this website.

🔎 Blade emotional computer

People have attacked self-driving cars in Arizona and security robots in San Francisco. And in a Japanese mall, groups of small children called a humanoid robot names and formed circles around it to block it from moving. To train kids to treat robots gently, in 2018, Naver Labs in South Korea built a large robotic turtle called Shelly. The robot would light up and move its head and legs when patted, but withdraw into its shell when handled roughly.

In addition to complications having to do with social robots, there are some other concerns about the ways robots have become integrated with human life.

- **Robots are taking jobs that used to be done by humans.**
Delivery van drivers, warehouse workers, and hospital staff are already being replaced by robots in some places. One study predicts robots will replace 800 million human workers worldwide by the year 2030.

- **Robots are invading people's privacy.**
Through AI and machine learning, robot brains collect a lot of personal information about their human owners. Security robots record where you shop. Digital assistants keep track of what you like to eat. And your robovac may be sending a map of your living room to companies that want to sell you things.

- **Robots are getting into accidents.**
As they move out of the laboratory and into the real world, robots are getting into trouble. A food delivery robot in California burst into flames. A security robot at an office complex tumbled into a courtyard fountain. And self-driving cars have crashed into walls, other vehicles, and people on the street.

Robot-Building Prodigy

Tesca Fitzgerald was the lead programmer on her First Robotics team at age five. At age 10, she came up with a unique way to fit more code in the team's robot that impressed international judges. And by 17, she started her PhD in artificial intelligence, working with the robot Curi at Georgia Tech.

Watch a video about Tesca's early achievements here.

Tesca made with code

PS

DESIGNING FRIENDLY ROBOTS

Engineer Carla Diana created the look of Simon and Curi. She gave them white plastic faces with large eyes and glowing, oval ears. Their cute features were meant to make people want to help them. But the engineer says many robots are social, even if we don't think of them that way.

Social robots don't have to be smart or look alive to be friendly. In 2008, New York artist Kacie Kinzer (1983–) set a cardboard "robot" called a Tweenbot loose in a city park to see how people would react. The Tweenbot carried a sign asking for help getting to the other side of the park. Many people stopped to turn the robot in the right direction or fix it when it got stuck. A few tried telling it where to go—even though it was just a cardboard box with motorized wheels and a drawn-on face.

Hear leading roboticists of today discuss what the future may bring on the Robots site of the engineering organization IEEE. **Then, check out the rest of the site to see photos and videos of amazing robot inventions!**

🔎 robots IEEE learn

PS

In 2008, a study by Saint Louis University found that Sony's robotic dog Aibo was as good as a real dog at cheering up the residents of a senior citizen home. The study showed that robots can make good pets for people who are not able to take care of real animals.

Another robotic pet, a baby seal named Paro, is specially designed for people in nursing homes. Developed by Japanese engineer Takanori Shibata, the furry robot helps patients relax when they are worried. It can recognize some words, make sounds like a real baby harp seal, and respond happily to praise and cuddling.

CAREBOTS are social robots that are used as **COMPANIONS** for older people and children.

Takanori has said he chose to make Paro look like a seal because most people have never seen a real seal up close. He believes patients are more accepting of a robotic seal than of a robotic dog or cat.

Stuart Caie (CC BY 2.0)

Robots are sure to become more common in everyday settings, and roboticists are working to make them safer, friendlier, and more helpful. According to Colin Angle (1967–), one of the inventors of the Roomba robotic vacuum, the science of robotics has advanced more in the past few years than in the previous 50! Robots are changing the world, and the people who design and build robots will play a big role in deciding what the future will look like. Maybe that will be you!

ESSENTIAL QUESTION

How might robots change the way we live in the future?

So, You Want to Build Robots . . .

If the simple robot projects in this book make you want to try more, you're in luck! There are many ways to get started in robotics. See if there's a robotics team in your school or area. Many colleges offer summer and weekend robotics camps and workshops for kids. And youth organizations such as the Girl Scouts and 4-H are adding robotics to their programs. Of course, you can always create robots on your own using kits or DIY projects in books and online. Here are some kits and competitions to check out. You'll find more robotics resources for beginners in the back of the book. Have fun seeing what kind of robots you can come up with!

> › VEX Robotics,
> vexrobotics.com

> › ProtoSnap MiniBot Kit, sparkfun.com

> › First Lego League, firstlegoleague.org

> › Botball, botball.org

> › Lego Boost
> lego.com/en-us/themes/boost

> › Lego Mindstorms, mindstorms.lego.com

> › Tech Will Save Us Micro Bot
> techwillsaveus.com/shop/microbit-microbot-kit

> › Dexter Gigglebot
> gigglebot.io

> › LittleBits Droid Inventor Kit,
> shop.littlebits.com/products/droid-inventor-kit

TEACH A ROBOT TO
PLAY NIMBLE

TOOLBOX!

° 2 players

° 3 clear plastic cups

° 13 game pieces, such as
  coins, pebbles, or marbles

° 45 game counters such as
  buttons, beads, or candy
  in red, yellow, and blue or
  any three different colors,
  about 15 of each color

NIMBLE—the Nim Box Logic Engine—is a machine learning engine that learns to play a math game called Nim. Software engineer Alishah Novin of Nashville, Tennessee, created a version for kids using cups and Starburst candies. You can use any kind of colored game counters.

In Nim, players take turns picking game pieces from a row of pieces. The player who picks the last piece loses. It's perfect for ML because if you start with a certain number of pieces and follow a secret rule, you will always win.

If you have never played Nim, try the game first by playing against a friend (or by playing both sides yourself). Then, see how many rounds it takes for NIMBLE to figure out the algorithm that guarantees victory!

1. To try a practice round of Nim, start with a row of five, nine, or 13 coins. Take turns picking either one, two, or three coins. The player left with the last marble loses. Can you figure out the secret rule? (To check your answer, see Page 107.)

2. Label the cups with the numbers 2, 3, and 4. In each cup, put six buttons, two of each color. Put the extra buttons in a pile on the side. One player, the robot, will make random choices by drawing a colored button out of one of the cups. The other player, the human, will follow the secret rule.

3. Set up a row of five coins. The human player goes first and takes one, two, or three coins.

4. Now, it is the robot's turn. Find the cup that shows the number of coins that are left in the row—2, 3, or 4. Close your eyes and choose a button out of that cup. Make your move depending on the color of the counter:

* red = take one coin

* yellow = take two coins

* blue = take three coins

5. Set the button you chose to the side. Continue the same way until one player wins and the round is over. If the robot wins, "reward" it for making the right choice by putting the button back in the cup it came out of and adding another button of the same color. If the robot loses, "punish" it by putting that button to the side.

6. Set up the row of coins again as in Step 3 and keep playing rounds the same way. The longer you play, the better the robot should get. With every round, the robot has fewer wrong color buttons and more right color buttons to choose from. That means it is more likely to choose the right color button. Its confidence that its answer is correct goes up. You can keep going until the robot is following the secret rule every turn. At that point, its confidence is 100 percent!

Try This!

Think about how to train the robot quicker by adjusting the rewards and punishments. Or figure out how the set-up would change if you tried training it on a row of nine coins. Do you know any other games you could teach a machine to play using AI?

Secret Rule: Let the other player go first. Whatever number they pick, you pick the number that together adds up to four. If they take three, you take one. If they take two, you take two, and so on. Why does it work? Because you started with a number that is one more than a multiple of four. In other words, you can break those numbers up into groups of four and always have one left over.

3-D printer: a machine or printer that creates three-dimensional objects using a range of materials.

accelerometer: an electronic component that uses gravity to tell how a device is tilted and how fast it is moving.

actuator: a piece of equipment that makes a robot move.

algorithm: a set of steps that are followed to solve a mathematical problem or to complete a computer process.

animatronic: an electronic puppet, often life-sized, that can move and speak pre-recorded sentences.

artificial intelligence (AI): the intelligence of a computer, program, or machine.

atoms: the extremely tiny building blocks that make up all matter.

attract: to pull toward.

augmented reality (AR): technology that adds images or text over a view of an actual place viewed through a device such as a smartphone camera.

automata: machines that can move by themselves (singular is automaton).

automated: run by machine rather than by people.

BCE: put after a date, BCE stands for Before Common Era and counts down to zero. CE stands for Common Era and counts up from zero. These non-religious terms correspond to BC and AD. This book was printed in 2019 CE.

binary system: a math system containing only zeroes and ones. It is used by computers to indicate whether a switch is on or off.

bioengineering: the use of engineering principles applied to biological function to build devices, tools, or machines for a human need.

biohybrid: a robot with living material added to it.

biomimetic: a machine or material that copies a living thing.

Bluetooth: the short-range wireless interconnection of mobile phones, computers, and other electronic devices.

Boolean logic: invented by British mathematician George Boole in 1847, it is a way to turn problems into true or false questions.

bug: a mistake in a computer program.

capacitor: an electrical component, such as a battery, that stores an electrical charge and releases it all at once when needed.

caster: a wheel or ball-shaped roller that can swivel to point in any direction.

centaur: a mythical creature with the lower body of a horse and the head and upper body of a human.

cerebral palsy: a brain condition that makes it difficult to move and maintain balance and posture.

chatbot: an AI program designed to have natural-sounding conversations with humans.

circuit: a path that lets electricity flow when closed in a loop.

clean room: a room in a laboratory or factory where objects that must be kept free of dust or dirt are made.

closed circuit: an electric circuit that provides an unbroken path for the flow of current.

cloud robotics: designing robots that require computing power or information from the internet to function.

computer: an electronic device that stores and processes information.

computer chip: another word for microprocessor.

computer program: a set of steps that tells a computer what to do.

conditional statement: also known as an if-then-else statement, a step in a program that gives a computer two choices depending on whether the answer to a certain test is true or false.

conductive: describes a material that carries electricity easily. Metal is conductive, as are most wet surfaces, including skin.

controller: a switch, computer, or microcontroller that can react to what the sensor detects.

crimping: connecting two pieces of metal by squishing them together.

crop: a plant grown for food or other uses.

current: the flow of electricity through a circuit.

cyborg: a human or animal that is part robot.

data: information, usually given in the form of numbers, that can be processed by a computer.

debug: going through a computer program to find and remove any mistakes.

deep learning: an area of machine learning that uses large amounts of data and finds ways to connect them.

defuse: to prevent something from exploding.

degrees of freedom: the number of directions in which a robotic effector or other part can move.

device: a piece of equipment, such as a phone, that is made for a specific purpose.

digital assistant: also called a smart speaker, a chatbot housed in a device that answers questions, plays music and games, and does tasks such as make phone calls, look up information, and control household electronics such as lights and alarms.

drive system: wheels, legs, or other parts that make a robot move.

drone: a plane, quadcopter, or other aircraft that can be controlled by a pilot on the ground.

effector: a device that lets a robot affect things in the outside world, such as a gripper, tool, laser beam, or display panel.

electricity: a form of energy produced by the movement of charged particles between atoms.

electromagnet: a magnet that can be turned on and off using electricity.

electronic: describes a device that uses computer parts to control the flow of electricity.

electron: one of the particles that make up atoms. It carries a negative charge.

element: a substance that is made of one type of atom, such as iron, carbon, or oxygen.

engineering: the use of science, math, and creativity to design and build things.

evolve: to change through time, sometimes into something more complex.

exoskeleton: a skeleton on the outside of a body.

feedback: information about the result of an action that is sent back to the person or machine that performed the action.

flowchart: a diagram of an algorithm.

function: a short piece of code that is given a name so it can be used multiple times in a program simply by inserting the name.

gravity: a force that pulls all objects toward the earth.

hacking: using electronics skills to make a device do something it was not designed to do.

hardware: the body, motors, and other physical parts of a robot or other device.

humanoid: a robot or creature shaped like a human being.

hybrid: something that combines two different things, such as a car that can use two different kinds of devices to power it.

hydraulic: a system that pushes and pulls objects using tubes filled with fluid.

hydrothermal vent: an opening in the ocean floor that releases hot gases and minerals from underground.

icon: a small picture that opens a tool, page, or file on a computer.

infrared (IR): a type of light with a longer wavelength than visible light. It can be felt as heat.

input: a signal or information that is put into a machine or electrical system.

insulation: material that slows or prevents electricity from flowing. Plastic, rubber, and paper can be used to insulate circuits.

Internet of Things (IoT): devices that can be connected to each other and controlled over the internet.

joint: a place on a robot arm or other part where it can bend or turn.

laser-cut: cut with a laser cutter, a programmable machine that uses a focused beam of powerful light to burn through wood, paper, metal, or other materials.

LED: tiny light bulbs used in many electronic devices.

lever: a bar or handle used to run or adjust something.

lidar: a device that measures distance by shining light at an object and measuring the time it takes for the light to reflect back.

logic gate: an electronic circuit that takes one or more inputs, analyzes them, and produces one output.

loop: a short piece of code that is repeated a certain number of times until a specific condition is met.

machine learning (ML): a form of AI that lets you train a computer to look for clues to the meanings of words and images. The ML program you create to analyze specific data is called a machine learning engine.

manipulate: to handle or control.

memory: the part of a computer where information is stored.

microcontroller: a very small device that works like a mini-computer.

microprocessor: a tiny electronic component that processes and stores information.

modular: robots that can work alone or be connected in different combinations to form a larger robot.

nanobot: a tiny robot, too small to see without a microscope.

NASA: National Aeronautics and Space Administration. The U.S. organization in charge of space exploration.

natural language processing: a branch of AI that helps computers understand and use human language.

nuclear: energy produced when the nucleus of an atom is split apart.

nucleus: the center of an atom.

open circuit: a circuit with a break in the path that prevents electricity from flowing.

open source: a computer program or device that makes its design information public so that others can help improve the design and make their own versions.

output: the movement or other response of a robot to the input it receives from its sensors.

plasma torch: a tool that uses streams of electrified gas to cut through sheets of metal.

pneubotics: inflatable robots made of air.

pneumatic: a system that pushes and pulls objects using tubes filled with air or other gases.

pollination: transferring pollen from the male part of a flower to the female part so that the flower can make seeds.

powered exoskeleton: a "robot suit" that can be worn to give a person added strength.

programmable: able to be provided with coded instructions for the automatic performance of a task.

prosthetic: an artificial body part, such as an arm or leg.

proton: one of the particles that make up atoms. It carries a positive charge.

prototype: a working model of something that allows engineers to test their idea.

proximity: how near something is.

pseudocode: a computer program written out in human words instead of special programming terms (pseudo means "fake").

punch card: a card with holes punched in it that gives directions to a machine or computer.

radar: a device that detects objects by bouncing microwaves or radio waves off them and measuring how long it takes for the waves to return.

radiation: energy in the form of waves or particles.

radioactive: a substance made of atoms that gives off nuclear energy.

radio transmitter: the part of a radio that sends signals.

repel: to push away.

resistance: the measure of how hard it is for electricity to flow through a material or a part in a circuit. An insulator has very high resistance. A variable resistor changes the amount of resistance depending on certain conditions.

resistor: an electronic component that limits the amount of electricity flowing through it.

robot: a machine that is able to sense, think, and act on its own.

roboticist: a scientist who works with robots.

robotics: the science of designing, building, controlling, and operating robots.

salvaged: a part saved from something that is broken or no longer used.

scavenged: taken from something that is broken or no longer used.

semiconductor: a material such as silicon that can vary the amount of electrical charge it will carry depending on certain conditions.

sense-think-act cycle: a decision-making process used by robots.

sensor: in robotics, a device to detect what's going on outside the machine.

servo: a motor that can be controlled electronically.

shaft: a short rod on a motor that spins.

shape memory alloy (SMA): a special combination of metals that has one shape when at one temperature but can be "trained" to remember its original shape at a different temperature.

short circuit: a direct connection between two points in a circuit that aren't supposed to be directly connected.

smart home: a house in which all electric devices are monitored or controlled by a computer.

smart material: a material that can be used to build robots that react to their surroundings through their bodies.

social robot: a robot designed to talk, play, or work with humans in a lifelike way.

soft robot: a robot with a flexible or changeable body that helps it respond to its surroundings.

solar cell: a device that converts the energy in light into electrical energy.

solenoid: an electromagnetic device that pushes a rod up and down.

sonar: a way to detect objects by bouncing sound waves off them and measuring how long it takes to detect an echo.

stability: how well something can stay in its proper position.

STEM: an acronym that stands for science, technology, engineering, and mathematics. STEAM is STEM plus art.

swarm: a large group that moves together, such as a swarm of bees.

switch: a device that controls the flow of electricity through a circuit.

technology: the tools, methods, and systems used to solve a problem or do work.

telepresence: a robotic device that uses video and other types of sensors and displays to let someone in one place act and feel like they are in a room someplace else.

tendon: a tissue in humans and other animals that connects muscles to bones.

tilt switch: a sensor that turns on an electrical device when it is tilted.

torque: the amount of force it takes to make something turn or spin.

transistor: an electronic component made of a solid piece of material that is used as an on/off switch in electronic circuits.

Turing test: a series of questions to test whether a computer can think like a human being.

turtle robot: a robot used to teach coding using simple instructions that tell it how to move around a grid.

ultrasonic: describes a sound too high for humans to hear.

ultraviolet (UV): a type of light with a shorter wavelength than visible light, also called black light.

Uncanny Valley: the point at which a robot looks almost real and becomes strange and frightening.

vacuum tube: an electronic component that looks like a light bulb. It was used as an on/off switch in early computers and other appliances.

virtual robot: a programmable animation on a computer screen.

voltage: the amount of electrical energy available to flow between two points in a circuit. It is measured in volts. Every electronic part in a circuit requires a certain amount of voltage to run.

warm-blooded: animals that can keep themselves warm with their own body heat, such as human, birds, and bears.

wearable technology: electronic devices that are built into clothing (also called e-textiles) or worn as accessories.

welding tool: a blowtorch or other device that joins two pieces of metal together by heating them until they melt.

Wi-Fi: technology that allows the wireless transmission of radio waves.

x and y coordinates: two numbers that give the position of a point on a grid of squares, where x is the horizontal distance (right or left) and y is the vertical distance (up or down) from a central point that is labeled zero.

Metric Conversions

Use this chart to find the metric equivalents to the English measurements in this book. If you need to know a half measurement, divide by two. If you need to know twice the measurement, multiply by two. How do you find a quarter measurement? How do you find three times the measurement?

English	Metric
1 inch	2.5 centimeters
1 foot	30.5 centimeters
1 yard	0.9 meter
1 mile	1.6 kilometers
1 pound	0.5 kilogram
1 teaspoon	5 milliliters
1 tablespoon	15 milliliters
1 cup	237 milliliters

BOOKS ABOUT ROBOTICS AND ROBOT BUILDING

Swanson, Jennifer. *National Geographic Kids Everything Robotics: All the Photos, Facts, and Fun to Make You Race for Robots.* National Geographic Children's Books, 2016.

McComb, Gordon. *Building Your Own Robots: Design and Build Your First Robot!* (Dummies Junior) For Dummies, 2016.

McComb, Gordon. *Robot Builder's Bonanza* (Fifth Edition). McGraw Hill Education TAB, 2018.

Platt, Charles. *Make: Easy Electronics.* Maker Media, 2017.

Ragan, Sean Michael. *Make: Breadboard Bots!* Maker Media, 2019.

ROBOTICS WEBSITES

IEEE Robots: *Information about robots and robotics for students from the world's largest technical professional organization.*
robots.ieee.org

The Robotics Alliance Project:
NASA's robotics website for students and the public.
robotics.nasa.gov

Robohub: *News about robotics research, start-ups, business, and education.*
robohub.org/category/learn

Soft Robotics Toolkit Created by Harvard:
Contains info, student resources, and hosts a yearly competition.
softroboticstoolkit.com

Science Buddies Project ideas for students and educators:
sciencebuddies.org/science-fair-projects/project-ideas/robotics

Instructables: *The how-to site has tons of tutorials for beginners on up.*
instructables.com

ROBOTICS KITS AND COMPETITIONS

VEX Robotics: vexrobotics.com

ProtoSnap MiniBot Kit: sparkfun.com

First Lego League: firstlegoleague.org

Botball: botball.org

Lego Boost:
lego.com/en-us/themes/boost

Lego Mindstorms: mindstorms.lego.com

Tech Will Save Us Micro Bot:
techwillsaveus.com/shop/microbit-microbot-kit

Dexter Gigglebot:
gigglebot.io

LittleBits Droid Inventor Kit:
shop.littlebits.com/products/droid-inventor-kit

QR CODE GLOSSARY

Page 8: youtu.be/XQ8tPOqN7WE

Page 24: mars.nasa.gov/mars2020

Page 29: wyss.harvard.edu/technology/programmable-robot-swarms

Page 31: news.nationalgeographic.com/2018/05/
robotic-living-muscle-tissue-science

Page 32: smithsonianmag.com/innovation/12-year-old-girl-
built-robot-can-find-microplastics-ocean-180970607

Page 33: robotmissions.org

Page 36: softroboticstoolkit.com/shape-memory-locomotion

Page 36: instructables.com/id/Soft-Robotic-Grabber-No-3D-Printer-Required

Page 41: youtube.com/watch?v=Pj-NqWDH2qE

Page 45: news.engin.umich.edu/2019/04/robotic-jellyfish-
research-wins-best-student-paper-award-at-spie-2019

Page 46: youtube.com/watch?v=2FBmH2QCTxM

Page 54: youtu.be/rgpf7Rcjf-g

Page 60: youtube.com/watch?v=T9nngOrdPkg

Page 65: media.mit.edu/projects/elowan-a-plant-robot-hybrid/overview

Page 69: techcrunch.com/2018/06/28/disney-imagineering-
has-created-autonomous-robot-stunt-doubles

Page 73: youtube.com/watch?v=BwKQ9Idq9FM

Page 79: el.media.mit.edu/logo-foundation

Page 80: lightbot.com

Page 82: hourofcode.com/us/learn

Page 86: scratch.mit.edu/projects/277983733

Page 86: yurisuzuki.com/archive/works/colour-chaser

Page 88: adafruit.com

QR CODE GLOSSARY (CONTINUED)

Page 90: makecode.com/_ceJ5gMTYJbH9

Page 90: makecode.microbit.org/_RehLFfLCdRH3

Page 93: makecode.adafruit.com

Page 93: learn.adafruit.com

Page 95: codeclubprojects.org/en-GB/scratch/chatbot

Page 97: machinelearningforkids.co.uk

Page 97: cognimates.me/home

Page 97: teachablemachine.withgoogle.com

Page 98: youtu.be/FPIaU8QJh3g

Page 101: youtu.be/a-S-Mc_rzCM

Page 102: youtu.be/2Viy2UFyb7U

Page 103: robots.ieee.org/learn

ESSENTIAL QUESTIONS

Introduction: What task would you ask a robot to do?

Chapter 1: Which robotic inventions do you think have helped humans the most?

Chapter 2: How does a robot's body help it do its job?

Chapter 3: How could new power sources help the development of better robots? What ideas do you have for unique ways to power robots?

Chapter 4: Why is it difficult to build robotic effectors that work as well as human arms and legs?

Chapter 5: Why do robots need so many different kinds of sensors?

Chapter 6: How is a computer program for a robot different from a step-by-step set of instructions?

Chapter 7: How might robots change the way we live in the future?

INDEX